The Haunting of Beech Grove

The Haunting of Beech Grove

The Story as Never Told Before

Richard H. Blankenship &
Shannon J. Johnson II

RESOURCE *Publications* · Eugene, Oregon

THE HAUNTING OF BEECH GROVE
The Story as Never Told Before

Resource Publications
An Imprint of Wipf and Stock Publishers
199 W. 8th Ave., Suite 3
Eugene, OR 97401

www.wipfandstock.com

PAPERBACK ISBN: 979-8-3852-5954-0
HARDCOVER ISBN: 979-8-3852-5955-7
EBOOK ISBN: 979-8-3852-5956-4

In loving memory of Nan,
without whose diaries,
this project would not exist.

The real Nancy and Joseph.

Contents

CONTENTS

Introduction

We moved into the house on Beech Grove Road in 1997. Never could we have dreamed that we would be living a nightmare that would not only test the faith and strength of our family, but threaten our very souls. It was here that we would face the torment of not knowing what would happen next, or to whom.

I never believed in the supernatural before, but I do now. Spirits are walking among us, but why, I don't know. I am convinced that there is something out there after we die: a life after death. What was waiting for us in the house, was nothing short of death itself, laying in wait to draw the life from our bodies. Journey now into the bone-chilling experience, taken from the pages of my own diary, of the tale of the haunted house on Beech Grove Road.

The Haunting

The house on Beech Grove Road came up for sale at a good time in our lives. Our house had just burnt down and my husband John and I, along with our daughter Sarah, had been living in a trailer without much room to spare. Our two older children were married with children of their own, and both had been pressing us to buy a proper house. I suppose the trailer didn't feel enough like home.

At first, I thought it was a bit hard to believe that the house was for sale again so soon; it was like no one was satisfied with it. It had been sold three times in the past ten years, not counting the renters that had been in and out. I figured it was partially due to most younger couples wanting a new home. I didn't care about that. It was a beautiful older home, and though I had only seen it from the road, I could easily see myself living happily there in idyllic peace.

John and I had been married nearly forty years at that time. We were only teenagers when we married, and had made it through a lot of happy times and a lot of heartache. We owned a trucking company that was named after the road we lived on, and I was working at the diner in town. Now, more than ever, we were in a position to buy the place we really wanted. Looking up at that house on the hill made me feel like we were starting fresh all over again.

The day after I had seen it was back for sale, John was off work and he called to make an appointment to go look at the house. To our surprise, we were able to get in to look it over the same day. As the realtor unlocked the door and we stepped inside, I noticed that the house was full of furniture, dishes, food, and everything, as if the home was still being occupied. I mentioned it to the real estate agent and asked if someone was still living there. "No." he replied, "When they left, they just left everything behind."

I had remembered that the previous time we looked at the house, there was an upright piano there. Looking around, I noticed it was gone. I asked the agent where it had went. He told us that there was a doctor who had been going through a divorce, and he was renting the house until he could find a more permanent place to stay. For some reason, one day the doctor pushed the piano into the basement, breaking every step in the process. After him, the current couple moved in and replaced the stairs with lumber from the husband's work.

As we went down into the basement, something shiny in one of the furthest corners caught my eye. I drew nearer to see what it was, only to discover that it was part of the upright piano. I thought of what a shame it was that this was all that was left of such a beautiful old piano. I couldn't fathom why he would have destroyed it. It would have been a lovely piece to have in the house.

After looking through the house, I just knew we had to buy it. The best part about it for me was the basement. I had always been afraid of storms, and now I would have a place to go, if needed. John and I talked for a few hours after we left. It was going to be a fair amount of work, but our desire to have it outweighed everything else. We signed the paperwork and moved into the house only a week later. I could hardly believe it, the house was finally ours.

2

After unpacking the last box, I sat with a cup of coffee on the porch to enjoy a moment of quiet. I found my mind going back to the couple that had moved out of the house. Why had they left everything there? Why didn't they come back to get them? Wouldn't they need their things wherever it was they moved to?

That night, I went to bed early, exhausted from moving their belongings out and ours in. At about three in the morning, I woke up to the sound of someone knocking at the door. "Who would be knocking at our door at this time of night?" I wondered. I got up out of bed and went to the door, but no one was there. I checked through the window and couldn't see anyone outside. Curious as to what, or who it might have been, I went back to bed, thinking I might find out in the morning. When morning came, I asked John if he had heard anything last night, but he said he hadn't. What did I hear? Did I dream it all?

3

I've noticed that since we moved in, my husband and I had been really tired all of the time. Whenever we were away from the house, we felt fine, but within an hour of returning, it was back to zero. We felt like every ounce of energy was being drained from us. It wasn't just us either. Any time we had someone over to the house, before long they would be feeling the same way as well.

In those days, we had carbon monoxide detectors in the house. I say had, because at the time, they would go off randomly throughout the day and night. I changed batteries and even took the batteries out, but still, against all logic and good sense, they would beep.

I started to think that maybe it was due to a gas or carbon monoxide leak, so I called the gas company to see if they would send someone out to check. To my relief, they sent someone out right away. Just to be on the safe side, he brought equipment to check for everything and anything that could be causing our problem. He carefully checked all over the house, but found nothing wrong. Once he was done, he gave me a paper saying that there weren't any leaks inside or out.

While I was glad to know that we didn't have any leaks, I didn't know what else it could be. Knowing the house was free of carbon monoxide though, I did come up with a solution for the troublesome detectors. I took a hammer and beat the confounded things off the wall: no more beeps. When my husband got home that evening, he was a little shocked to find out the news regarding the inspection results. One possibility down, we had to continue to wonder what might be the cause of our problems.

4

I was beginning to wonder if we had made the right choice buying the house. I decided to clean the bathroom after everyone had gotten cleaned up, and as I was cleaning the mirror, I noticed a shadow behind me. It was thick and dark, and moved like a wave of smoke. As I stared at the shadow in the reflection, I could swear I saw in it the face of an older man. I could see the movement of his eyes as he kept looking up and down.

I could feel cold chills creeping up the back of my neck as I made eye contact with him. In the blink of an eye, the shadow shot straight up through the ceiling and was gone. I stood in front of the mirror looking at myself; I couldn't believe what I just saw. If I told my husband about this, he would think I was crazy. There had to be an explanation, but what? Could there be a natural explanation for what I had seen? I didn't know if I'd be able to go back into the bathroom without wondering if I'd see it again. Why couldn't I forget his eyes? I couldn't let it get to me. I had no choice but to live in this house.

Later on, I decided to confide in my daughter Sherry, all the things that had been going on. I told her about the shadows and the knocks, but she didn't believe that it was anything to be taken serious.

"Oh mom!" She laughed. "It's an old house. You're bound to hear things that you can't explain. As far as being tired, you and pop have been going non-stop for days. Just give it some time and get settled in, and you'll see, everything will be fine." I hoped so.

5

Having gotten some of the more major repairs and cleaning done, we went about making the house more of our own by doing some painting. Sarah had been begging from the word "go" for us to let her have the basement as her room. So, as soon as we had time, we got the basement all cleaned up and ready to paint. The only thing that was left was the remnants of the old piano. It was going to take at least three stout men to get that out, being as heavy as it was.

The first day we had a chance, and Sarah wasn't in school, we went to town so she could pick out the paint for the basement. While in town, Sarah convinced us we had to stop at the mall so she could get a new CD. Her growing collection of music that I had no interest in listening to is one of the reasons I agreed to let her have the basement for her own. Thank God for earphones!

As we were leaving the mall, I heard someone call out, "Hey you!" Not thinking they were talking to me, I kept walking. "Hey you!" They shouted again. I turned around to see who was calling out. I recognized the person right away as the doctor who had lived in our house; the same that pushed the piano downstairs.

"Are you talking to me?" I asked.

He nodded his head. "Did you just move into the house on Beech Grove Road?" he asked in a serious tone.

I told him that we did. I was instantly curious about how exactly he knew we lived there. His demeanor seemed off: things were definitely not well with him.

"What about the basement?"

"What do you mean, 'what about the basement?'" I was beginning to get scared.

Before he had a chance to answer, his brother, who apparently was looking after him, came over to bring him back to their car. As they were walking away, he kept looking back at me. Besides being thoroughly creeped out, I also found it quite sad. This doctor was a well known and respected specialist in town, and now he was just a shell of a man. What happened to him?

Doing our best to put the incident at the mall out of our minds, we worked hard to get the basement painted. To Sarah's credit, it looked really cute once it was all done. Everyday after that, we would be lucky to see her after school. She would get off the bus and head straight for the basement until supper time. Down there, she had her phone, TV, computer: her own little world.

6

The house had been quiet for a few days, with hardly any activity at all. One evening, Sarah came home from school, and that rapidly and drastically changed. She went straight to the basement, like always, when she got in. She had a new CD that she couldn't wait to listen to. Sarah had only been down there for a few minutes when I heard her screaming. Thinking she saw a mouse or spider, I ran down to where she had been laying on the couch.

She looked up at me with a glare of bewilderment and panic and said, "Someone just laid on top of me! It took my breath and I couldn't breathe. As I was trying to get free, I felt someone lick my face. I could feel their tongue as it went up my face."

Thinking maybe someone had slipped past me up the stairs, I went around and searched the whole house, only to find no one. I asked if perhaps she had fallen asleep and dreamed the whole experience, but she was adamant that it was real. After this, she moved to an upstairs bedroom and would only go down into the basement if she had her friends with her.

7

It had got to the point where I was hearing something nearly every night: knocking on the basement door, someone running up and down the basement stairs, always something. Due to all of this activity, I could hardly sleep at night. We had been living in the house for about three months, when one night, I got up to watch some television. Just another, in a long line of nights without rest.

So I didn't wake my husband by watching TV in the bedroom, I decided to go to the living room.

I walked down the hall to the door of the living room. Standing there, looking for the remote, I could see the shadow of someone moving behind me in the light of the hallway. Startled, I turned around to see who was there: no one. I then turned quickly back to the living room, the hair standing on the back of my neck. My heart was pounding in my chest as I broke out in a cold sweat. Peering into the dim living room, I froze solid in fear of what I saw. There was a shadow moving from one wall to the next, like someone drawing a curtain closed. In the span of only a few frigged breaths, the whole room was engulfed in a darkness as black as pitch.

Breaking loose from the terror before me, I ran down the hall, jumping into the safety of my bed. My husband shot upright, startled by the movement.

"What's going on?" he asked.

"Turn on the light, quick!"

He got up and turned on the lights. "My God, Nancy! You look like you've seen a ghost."

I told him what happened, not expecting him to believe me. He walked down to the living room, but of course, no one and nothing was all he found.

8

Another night, my husband and I decided we would have a night alone. We rented movies, popped popcorn, relaxed, and tried to take our minds off of things. We were half way through the first movie when my husband nudged me to look towards the doorway of our bedroom. The hallway light was on and we could clearly see a shadow coming down the hall, blocking out the light more with each movement.

Without a word being said between us, we sat up quietly in bed and watched in anticipation. As the shadow drew slowly near, it soon stopped just before reaching our door. Slowly, it appeared to lean over as if trying to listen. My husband quickly jumped up and went towards the door. As he did, the shadow withdrew and was gone in an instance. We went through the house looking high and low to see if we could find the source of this shadow. All the doors and windows were locked and there was no one inside but us. Unable to find anyone or any thing, we went back to our movies, but it was the shadow that was on our mind.

9

A little while after this, my sister Daisy came to visit. It was great to see her as she always had a way of making someone feel better. After all the three of us had been through at the house, I was certain that having her stop by would be a breath of fresh air for us all. I hadn't seen or heard from Daisy for about a week, which wasn't like her at all. We were from a big family and she's the oldest of us all, and therefore was the most motherly.

When she arrived, I noticed that something was different about her. She looked like she had lost a lot of weight, and she certainly wasn't her usual happy-go-lucky self. A few years back, her and her husband had bought the farm we grew up on, and she had been ecstatic over it. I could hardly remember the last time I had seen her so happy.

That day, it looked like she was the one that needed perking up. Being that we're big coffee drinkers in our family, I made a pot and poured her a cup. I offered her some in a bid to get her to open up. Something was wrong, and she couldn't have hid it even if she tried. She looked devastated and utterly broken.

"I know something is wrong." I told her. "What is it?"

"We're selling the farm." She said, holding back tears. "And Steve wants a divorce."

Apparently, he had met someone else. In between wanting to march right over and have a serious talk with her husband, I could feel her pain. She had been keeping all of this to herself until the last minute, when things were past fixing. Of course, looking back,

I don't know if there was anything we could have done other than offer her our support. Perhaps that would have been enough.

I suggested she come and stay with us for a while, but she didn't want to. I was concerned about her being alone at that time. Daisy was the type of person who didn't want to feel like she was imposing on her family. She was always the caretaker, as I said: the motherly type. At that time, more than ever, I wanted her to know that no matter what, she had her family that loved her and was there by her side.

10

After having finally talked her into it, Daisy had come to stay with us for a few weeks. She was in the middle of a divorce and I had asked if she would stay with John and I for a while. It was a time when she needed her family close by to lean on. I just knew that after a while she would be back up and on her feet. She always was one of the strongest among us. Besides, having her around would be like old times. I just hoped I could help her in her time of need.

11

I noticed Daisy wasn't sleeping at night. I could hear her walking around the house at odd hours through the night. When I asked her about having trouble sleeping, she told me she had been sleeping alright. I wanted to believe her, but I knew something was amiss. Things only got worse when she barely would eat anything. When I would try to get her to eat, she would start gagging with every bite. In no time, she had lost a lot of weight. I chocked it all up to everything she was going through. Never-the-less, I was really worried.

12

Not long after she moved in, I was out on the front porch having coffee when Daisy came out and asked if I was in her room the night before. She said she could remember me talking to her, but couldn't remember what I had said or what I wanted. I told her it wasn't me, but maybe it was Sarah. When Sarah got up later on, I asked what she wanted with her aunt the night before. "I don't know what you are even talking about." she said. "I never left my room last night." After that, Daisy didn't want to talk anymore about it.

13

Late one night, after we all went to bed and the house was quiet, my husband and I were woke up by a loud, blood-curdling scream from Daisy's room. We both got up and scrambled to her room where she was sitting bolt upright in bed with a shocked look on her face. I asked if she was alright, she said she was, but she didn't want to talk about it. Thinking she must have had a nightmare, I laid my hand on her back to comfort her. When I did, I could feel that her whole body was trembling. Not knowing what else to do, I sat in silence with her until she could go back to sleep. Her sleep wasn't to last long though, as later on I could hear her walking through the house. Thinking that maybe now she would want to talk, I got up only to find her in bed. "Maybe in the morning she'll want to talk." I thought. Thinking no more of it, I went back to bed.

The next morning, I was sitting at the kitchen table having a cup of coffee when Daisy got up. I poured her a cup as she sat down in the place across from mine. After a few passing moments of silence, I gently asked what happened the night before. The look that came over her face worried me. She slowly leaned in and quietly said, "Nancy, there's something in this house." In disbelief, I asked her to clarify what she just said. "Last night when you heard me scream, there was someone in my room by the bedroom door, and he spoke to me again."

"Again?" I asked. In barely more than a whisper, she said, "I don't want you to think that I'm crazy, but the night that I thought you were in my bedroom, wasn't the only time that I've experienced things here. I've also seen *it* in the living room, and it's talked to me too."

I couldn't believe what she was saying. I knew my sister well, she wouldn't just make up something like this, knowing it would scare me. She would, however, be sure to warn me if she suspected my family or I were in danger. Entranced by her words, I let her continue to talk, though she seemed hesitant, as if she were afraid to get caught speaking to me. Frightened, but spurred on by curiosity and a desire to help, I asked her more about what happened and what exactly she saw.

"It was a shadow; darker than the dark. It looked like the devil himself, horns and all." she said, with a look of terror. "The first time it talked to me, I couldn't move. I was so scared. I could only stare until it walked into the closet and disappeared."

Her voice trembled out of the fear of even recalling the event. She went on to tell me that it told her not to be afraid. The darkness reassured her that it was her friend and that it wanted to help her. I asked her what it could help her with, but she said she didn't know.

Regaining some of her composure, Daisy said that she had a bad feeling about the house, and thought it would be best if we moved out. I explained that everything we owned was tied up in the house and we couldn't move if we wanted to. She insisted that we should at least have the house blessed, just to be safe. I didn't feel like she told me everything. All I could think of was what she *had* told me, and I worried what could be coming next.

14

I got up early the morning Daisy left. Sarah was preparing to leave for a week and go off to camp. I wanted to make sure she didn't forget to pack anything she might need. About six o'clock the following morning, I heard a faint knock at the door while I was in the bathroom. Not knowing what it was, I continued on with what I was doing and listened for a second knock.

As I went to the kitchen, I looked out the window over the sink just in time to see Daisy's car starting down the driveway. I started to run to catch her before she got too far, but before I got outside, she had already gone. I was curious what she could have wanted this early in the morning, and why she didn't stay. I figured that it must not have been very important, and that we would talk about it later. That day was our youngest brother Frank's birthday party. It was a tradition of ours to get together on each other's birthday and celebrate. Each birthday was a guaranteed time of year when we could take a break from our busy lives and catch up with each other. After dropping Sarah off for camp, John and I went to my mother's house for the party.

By the time we arrived, everyone was already there except Daisy. That wasn't like her to be late. Typically, she was the first one to arrive. After a few hours had past, she still hadn't arrived. Thinking that maybe she had car trouble, we made calls and drove around anywhere we thought she might be, but we never found her.

It really bothered me, this wasn't like Daisy at all. John and I had talked to her on the phone a few days prior. She was still whispering; a fact that struck us both as odd. As before, I asked her why she was talking so hushed. "He might hear us." Was all she would say, never elaborating on who "he" was. The only other thing she would tell us was that she had to protect her family. Again, from who or what, she would never say. These details omitted, it was still enough to scare me and make me worry for her.

After the party, still not able to find her, we decided to go home and wait for her to call one of us. I had gone into the living room and was watching TV, while John was sitting at the kitchen table doing some much needed paperwork for the trucking company. As he worked, he was listening to his police scanner. It was getting quite late, around half-past ten, when he called out to me, telling me what he just heard.

On the scanner, he said, they had just found a car up at the cross with a suicide note in it. I wondered if it was anyone we knew. The cross sits up on Fort Jefferson Hill; so named for the old Civil War fort that sat up there. The site is marked by a ninety foot tall cross that sits above the Mississippi River, and can be seen from three states: Kentucky, Missouri, and Illinois.

Soon after the report of the car came over the radio, our phone started to ring. I hoped to myself that it was Daisy calling to tell us she was alright and explain her absence that day. My husband picked up and began to listen intently: it wasn't Daisy. I noticed that as he spoke, he kept his voice low. He hung up the phone and it rang again. After hanging up, he asked me to come into the kitchen and have a seat at the table. I could feel in my gut that it was bad news.

He pulled out a chair so I could sit next to him. About the same time, my daughter Sherry and her best friend came walking through the door. I knew without a doubt that whatever happened was terrible. Having searched for the words, my husband broke the news: the car and the suicide note were Daisy's. I didn't want to believe it. I could do nothing but fall to pieces.

My mind painfully raced back to that morning when I heard the knock on the door. Had she been there to talk to me? Had she came to say goodbye? Could I have stopped her somehow? My mind was in a frenzy trying to imagine a scenario that would have made things any different. I knew that I would blame myself for the rest of my life. That same night, the police brought us her suicide note to make sure the handwriting was hers: it was.

15

The next three days were like living a nightmare I couldn't wake up from. Each moment of every day, I felt like I was walking around in a daze. I read her suicide note over and over. I noticed that at the last part of the note, the post script, was different. It was at that point that you could see her hand had started shaking. Her note read:

"It's nobody's fault. My body is in so much pain: there's no cure.

P.S. I'm in the river."

True to her word, they found her in the river the third day. Her autopsy would show that there was nothing about her body that would have caused her to be in a great deal of pain.

The torrent of questions that poured through my mind seemed to be without end. Why didn't I see what she was going through? Why didn't I insist she explain who "he" was that she was afraid of? Why did I let her keep whispering in fear every time we talked? Could I have stopped her? All these things and more I wondered, knowing she took the answers to her grave. I'll never know, and that alone is enough to haunt anyone.

16

More than a week since her death, and I still haven't found my way fully back to reality. I go to her grave every day. It kills me to know we were unable to dress her and embalm her properly for her burial, due to how long she was in the river. All we could do is lay her to rest in a body bag, in her casket. Just another series of thoughts to torment my exhausted mind.

One day, as I sat beside her grave, I started to clean off the flowers that had died so I could replace them. That's when I was hit with an awful smell. Perhaps it was my imagination, but it certainly seemed too real for me. I knew instantly what the smell was: it was Daisy's body decomposing beneath me. I went into a fit.

My husband had to drag me away to the truck as I melted into a horrified ball of tears. He tried to convince me that it was something else, but I knew what it was. The smell even seemed to be on my hands from touching her flowers. The whole incident left me scarred and sickened to my core.

17

I'm beginning to worry that I may be losing my mind. Last night, before I even laid my head down, I saw Daisy. As clear as the day is bright, I could see her face in front of me for a few seconds. I laid in bed most of the night, restless, just hoping she would come back. As I searched the darkness, I could hear footsteps, just like when she was staying with us. It sounded like Daisy was walking around like she did when she couldn't sleep. Up and down the hallway, the steps could be heard, as I finally fell asleep, my sister on my mind. I wonder, looking back, if it was really her spirit, or if it was the dark spirit trying to make me think it was her. What better way to get to me?

Her words continued to weigh on my mind, even well after the funeral. As time passed, I eventually got to the point where sleep was impossible until it got to be late in the night. I knew that she was telling me the truth, as I had begun to see the shadows too. It was hard enough for me to process, but as my little grandchildren grew, they were full of questions about what had happened. They didn't understand, and truthfully, neither did I. I didn't want them to know what really transpired. I didn't want to tell them that Daisy took her own life.

18

I knew it couldn't just be me seeing all these apparitions and hearing all of these noises, especially after what happened to Daisy. There was something happening in this house to one degree of intensity or another almost everyday. I wondered if whatever was in the house wanted us out like the rest of the couples that had lived here. Since we had done all of this work, it was almost like we'd woke something up out of the woodwork.

John and I were both still tired all of the time. When John wasn't at work, he would be in bed resting. It seems that since we started living at the house, we hadn't had a really happy moment. At times, I would really have liked to leave this place, but I knew we couldn't. The trucking company and everything else we had was intertwined with this house.

Why was this happening to us? Had someone died in the house or on the property, I wondered. I felt like I was going crazy. I mean, ghosts, things that go bump in the night, only crazy people encounter these: right? Crazy or not, I worried that just as this thing had convinced Daisy to kill herself, it might talk one of the grand-kids or someone else into doing something harmful. I simply couldn't let this happen.

No matter how hard I tried, it was really hard for me to believe in something "supernatural." Even so, I had seen the shadows, heard the knocking during the night, and heard someone or something going up and down the basement steps. I thought about everything that had happened since we moved in to the house. I noticed it mostly happened at night. More than any of that, I couldn't get Daisy out of my mind.

I thought of the promise that I made Daisy, all that time back, about getting the house blessed. I should have done it right after that first incident, or sooner, but I hadn't. After what happened with Daisy, and the recent up-tick in activity, I thought of calling our pastor before something else bad happened. I hesitated as I went for the phone. Being in a small town in the "Bible Belt," it doesn't take long for word to get around about anything. It certainly may not be right, but it was enough to cause concern.

19

It was the events that happened on the following day that ended up dispelling all of my concerns for worldly regards. There was a severe storm warning out, so my daughter Sherry and her kids came to stay with us until everything quieted down. Like myself, she is also scared of storms. Right after they got there, the kids wanted to watch TV. So Sherry went to my room to watch the weather and keep an eye on things. It hadn't been long before she started calling, wanting me to come into the bedroom.

Not wanting to alarm me that something had happened, she talked in a hushed tone. She told me she had been shocked while she was laying in the bed. I couldn't really believe that, as there was nothing in my bed that could shock her. Even after having been told this, she insisted, saying it felt like something had shocked her in the back. More than this, she said that when it happened, the foot of the bed shook as well.

She told me that it was all she could do to keep from screaming when it happened. Not knowing what else to say, I told her that I had been thinking of having the house blessed. Sherry told me that until I did, she didn't want the kids spending the night, in case something were to happen to them. Right then and there, with Sherry beside me, I called our pastor. There was no way that anything was going to keep me from my grandchildren.

20

One night soon after, was the most afraid I had every been in that house. I decided to take a hot bath, hoping it would help me sleep better. While laying back in the tub, the shampoo bottle started to rock back and forth. It rocked back and forth about five or six times before it stopped. I knew I wasn't alone in the tub, and not knowing what might happen next, I got out of the tub and got ready for bed.

I got to bed a little later than my husband, which was typically how it went. John was already asleep by the time I got there. I had only just laid my head on my pillow, nowhere near being asleep yet, and I found myself frozen. I couldn't move anything. I could feel John laying there beside me, but I couldn't reach out to touch him or call out his name.

It was then that I saw him; some inhuman, dark form, that appeared to be like the devil himself. Large horns, like a ram, curled back on his head. His muscular frame could only just be made out; shaded in hues of black. I could only see him from the waist up from where I lay paralyzed, clutched in fear. I couldn't make out his face, not that I'm too sure I wanted to. I tried to convince myself that I was dreaming or having some terrible nightmare. "This can't be happening," I thought, but there was no reasoning with whatever was happening.

As I stewed in my panicked thoughts, I heard him speak. "Don't be afraid. I want to be your friend. I can help you; I helped Daisy, and I can help you too. Here, let me show you some of what I can do." He spoke in a soft tone, but his voice was deep and harsh, like one scorched by the thick smoke of hell's fire.

Petrified, I immediately found myself able to see things through his eyes. He took me to the basement, where Sarah and her friends were spending the night. It seemed like I was peaking at them through a crack in the wall. He showed me what the girls were doing: listening to music, talking on the phone, and looking up things on the computer they shouldn't.

"Look at how they're sleeping." he said. "That's how you'll know what I've shown you is true."

At 3:00 a.m. on the dot, he released me. I got out of bed as quick as I could and got dressed. I shook my husband awake, heart pounding out of my chest, and with one finger to my lips to keep him quiet, motioned for him to get dressed and come with me. I can still see his eyes as they snapped open, and the following look of confusion.

We left the house and drove down the road a ways before he pulled over and inquired as to what was going on. I knew how absurd what I was going to say would sound when I told him, but I had to tell him the truth. After I had told him everything that had happened, I told him I knew he didn't believe me, but it was the God's honest truth. To my great surprise, he said, "Yeah, I do."

At that moment, my mind raced back to the girls in the basement. I told John, we needed to get back to the house; I needed to make sure the girls were okay. As I slowly walked down each step into the basement, I could feel my legs getting weak. The first thing I noticed was that, just like in the vision, the lights were all on. I suppose Sarah must not have felt as scared with the lights on. Peering across the room, I could see the most significant proof that what I had seen had actually happened. Two of the girls were laying on the couch, one on each end, and the third was asleep on the floor next to them.

I stared in disbelief for a while before going back up stairs. My husband had a cup of coffee waiting for me at the kitchen table. As we sat there, trying to process everything that had happened, we heard a noise coming from somewhere in the house. We barely moved as we listened. Finally, John softly asked if I had called our pastor.

I was hating the idea that he was about to leave for work with all that was still going on. After he left, I sat in the kitchen, uneasy and alone. I thought about the tape recorder that my daughter Sherry had given me. I grabbed it from the drawer and put a new tape and batteries in it. Walking quietly down the dim hallway, I went into my bedroom, set it down, and pressed 'record' before going back to the kitchen. After about ten minutes, I went back to get it, at which point, I found the batteries were dead. I replaced them with another set and prepared to try again.

This time I decided to stay in the room. Everything was pitch black with the door closed, and I was scared to death. I held the recorder out away from me and started to ask questions. I asked if anyone was there, what their name was, and all of the other typical inquiries. I felt a bit silly sitting alone in a room talking to the air. After I finished, I hurriedly turned on the lights so I could listen to the recording.

At first, there was a whole lot of nothing, that is, until I asked for a name. Though I hadn't heard anything in the moment, I could clearly hear a man's voice reply on the recording. It sounded like a southern accent coming from someone that was standing right beside me. His voice sounded like that of a younger man; it was warm and kind. All I could make out was the phrase, "Prisoner 910." It must have been what he was known as at the time of his death. "What was his real name?" I wondered.

School got out and Rachel, who was only five at the time, came to visit. Being the sweet little girl she is, she thought that if she stayed with me, it would help me to feel better: it did help. She even would sleep with me and her papa. I was hoping we could use her visit as an opportunity to teach her to swim.

I like spending one-on-one time with each of my grandchildren whenever I can, and I want them all to have good memories of us and our house. For this, and nearly every other conceivable reason, we don't talk about the things that go on here in front of our grand-kids. The last thing we want is for anything to happen to them, or for them to become afraid of visiting their Nannie and Papa.

Finally, pool time came. Tired of being the only one of her rough and rowdy siblings who didn't know how to swim, Rachel was ready to master the water. We worked hard through most of the late morning and early afternoon. I was proud at how well she picked it up. After a while, we sat on the pool deck and took a break.

Though she was old enough for a regular cup, she still loved her sippy-cup, because it kept her from spilling anything on her favorite bathing suit. I told her that even if she spilled her juice on her, she would be able to wash it right off in the pool. This wasn't a good plan in her mind, and I didn't see the point in arguing.

Having gave in, I left Rachel in the swing by the pool where I could keep an eye on her while I got her cup. It only took me a couple of minutes until I got back. I handed her sippy-cup to her and sat down on the swing with her. She kept trying to talk in between sips, until she gave up and drank her fill of juice. Wiping her mouth, she excitedly asked, "Who was that girl that was standing in the yard? She was wanting me to play with her."

I got up and walked around a bit trying to find any sign of who she was talking about. I tried to tell her that no one was there, or had been there, the best I could tell. She remained adamant about what she had seen. "Nannie, she was there and she wanted to play." I told her that I couldn't imagine who it could have been. There wasn't even a family living near us that had a little girl. As much as I wanted to believe my granddaughter, I knew there was no one there because I could see her and the yard when I went for our drinks.

The more I tried to reason with her and explain that there wasn't a little girl there, the more adamant she got. Finally, I asked her what the girl looked like. She began to get excited then, thinking I was going to find her so they could play. I imagined that only having brothers to play with, a girl her own age would be a welcomed relief. Rachel told me she was wearing a pink dress and had beautiful, curly yellow hair. She also said that the girl had socks that went up to her knees. "Do you think she was going to a party, Nannie?" She asked.

As a way to settle her mind, I told that might be. "Perhaps that's why she left." I said. "Maybe she was heading to a party and didn't want to be late."

Far from settled, Rachel replied, "But she wanted me to go with her. She kept trying to get me to go and play with her. She was so pretty, Nannie. She looked like an angel."

As she went on and on about the little girl, chills began to run up my back. The only little girl that I could think of that looked like the child Rachel was describing, was my husband's niece. She sadly had died back in the early seventies: she was only seven years old. I was stretching my mind, trying to think of how Rachel would know about her.

My mind reeling, I thought about another horrid possibility: what if the demon, or whatever evil was here, was trying to trick her? Knowing that the form of a little girl would be a good way to deceive her, perhaps that was its way of luring her in. After all, it says in scripture that the devil can masquerade as an angel of light: how much easier would it be to appear as a child?

From this experience, I knew that I couldn't leave the kids alone, not even for a minute. Having lost interest in swimming, I decided we needed to go back in the house. I told Rachel that we could go back out later on that afternoon. As I was fixing her something to eat, she said, "Nannie, I wonder what made her shine."

Intrigued by her words, I told her that maybe the sun shinning off of her blonde hair made her shine. She shook her head at this and said that wasn't it, and that the girl had shined all over. I really didn't want to discuss the little girl anymore, but trying to change the subject was next to impossible. Rachel really felt that she had found a friend in this little girl. I thought that if a little girl was all it was, then there wasn't any real problem, but if it was anything more significant, there was a very grave problem. "How to tell the difference?" I wondered.

22

Another morning while she was staying with us, I was standing in the kitchen making my coffee. When she got up, I noticed she looked tired.

"Rachel, did you get enough sleep last night?" I asked. "It's still early sweetie, why don't you go back to bed?"

"No, Nannie." she replied. "I'm not ever going to spend the night with you again."

I could tell that she was being serious. So I, both a little hurt and confused, asked her why.

"Because you scared me last night."

Even more confused now, I asked her how I had scared her. I reassured her that I wouldn't do anything to scare her, and that I loved her and didn't want her to be afraid of anything in this world. I had to coax it out of her a little, but finally she told me what it was that frightened her.

"I woke up because I had to use the bathroom, and I saw you standing at the foot of the bed. Then I saw someone else standing behind you. Who was that? I called your name, but you wouldn't answer me."

Perplexed, I asked her, "Rachel, are you sure you weren't dreaming?"

"No, Nannie." She said confidently. "I woke up because I had to use the bathroom. I was sitting up in bed looking at you. You remember when you had long hair? Well, your hair was long again. How did you do that?"

I asked her if that was all she could remember. She then added that the figure she had seen had multi-color horns and the rest of it was darker that the rest of the room. This one chilling detail told me that what she saw was the same thing that Daisy had seen. Rachel asked me who it was behind me, and how I was able to be both there and in bed at the same time. She said that when she noticed this, was when she really got scared.

Not knowing what else to tell her, I told her that maybe it was an angel sent to watch over us as we slept. I didn't want to lie, but I knew that whatever it was, wasn't good. I thought to myself that whatever is in this house was going to continue to plague us until we ended up leaving like the other couples before us.

23

Our pastor should be here sometime this week to bless the house. I'm desperately hoping that after he comes, we'll be able to live a normal life free from the terrors that have plagued us. A few weeks ago, I've started to keep the TV on while we sleep, because it seems we don't hear as much when it's on. I remember sitting on the front porch, wondering about this small town of ours. I am beginning to believe that it's not just our home that is haunted. It is my considered opinion that this whole town is. Mainly, I think people just don't pay attention to it, or they don't talk about it out of fear of becoming marginalized.

I then began to think about my childhood. As a child, I wasn't really afraid of anything, that is, except the house mama and daddy bought in town after they sold the farm. It was there that I learned that there is more to existence than what we can physically experience. While I never saw anything there myself, my sister Ruth was tormented nightly by whatever was there. For years, my older sister Ruth was haunted by a man that would appear to walk through the house. It was nothing unusual to be woke up during the night by her screams.

To my recollection, there was only once that I remember hearing the man that haunted her. I was about nine years old then. Her, my brother Pat, and myself were the only ones home that night. I don't remember where the rest of the family went, but I remember distinctly what took place that night. My brother and sister were playing cards. I didn't know how, so I just sat and watched until I started getting sleepy. Ruth suggested I lay across the bed, but warned me not to take my shoes off. I remember thinking it was an odd request, especially since I knew you weren't supposed to wear shoes in bed.

After laying down, I was awoke at some point in the night by my sister putting my shoes back on. I was further alarmed by the sight of a shotgun laying on the bed beside me. Frightened, I looked over to see my brother who was holding a shotgun as well, and was trembling with fear. With how he was shaking, I was worried he might drop the shotgun.

Turning back to my sister, who was putting my other shoe on, I could hear a terrible racket from the other room. I knew then that we were not alone in the house. It sounded like whoever was in there was furious and tearing the house down. I could hear as things were being thrown against the wall and glass was shattering across the floor. I whispered to my sister and asked her what was going on. "It's him, and he's really mad." was all she would reply.

We hastily left the house, shotguns in hand, and walked across town to my aunt's house. We never found out more about the man that terrified Ruth. She would tell us that he would walk from room to room as if looking for someone, or something. Besides this, she would tell us, he always seemed upset. We lived at that house in town, until one by one, we got married and moved away, leaving far behind the memory of the man. Since then, Ruth would never speak about what happened then. I often wonder if she still thinks about it all.

After my own children were old enough to start school, my husband and I moved back to my home town in west Kentucky. If for no other reason, I thought it would be special for them to go to the same school that I had gone to. Also, around the same time, my brothers and sisters had also moved back and I wanted to be close to family. Since moving back, and moving onto Beech Grove Rd, I have to wonder if the man that tormented my sister those many years ago, is one of the troubled spirits haunting my home now.

24

The time had finally come for our pastor to come and bless the house. We talked about everything that had been going on over coffee before getting started. We began with having prayer. Before moving on to the blessing, he excused himself to use the bathroom. Coming out of the bathroom, he told us that he could feel the effects of whatever was present in the house. He said he could tell that what was occupying the home clearly knew what he was there for and was threatened. The whole time he was in the bathroom, he said he wasn't able to shake the hair-raising feeling that he was being watched.

We proceeded with the house blessing, and almost immediately, it felt like everything was lighter. I personally felt better knowing that I finally had fulfilled my promise to Daisy. Now, I hoped we could live in the house we worked so hard for without being afraid. Before our pastor left that night, he made the statement that he thought the spirit in the house was pure evil and if he was us, he would move. Less than reassured, we knew that wasn't going to be possible.

25

We had been invited out to our pastor's house after church for a visit a couple of nights after he blessed the house. In the course of our conversation, we got on the topic of our house. I had heard him preach multiple times on evil and the fallen angels. He had said, "I know it's hard for some people to believe that demons roam the earth, but if you believe in God, you have to believe in demons. It's in the Bible, and everything in the Bible is the truth."

Apparently, my husband felt inspired, or perhaps, comfortable enough to share, because that night was the first time I had heard him speak of things that he had experienced in the house. He seldom talked about his private matters, and almost never talked about the house or what was going on inside.

He shared with us that one evening, he had made himself a cup of coffee and went to the bedroom to sit in bed, relax, and watch TV. After a while, he said he turned the TV off and closed his eyes. He told us that he wasn't yet asleep when he felt the bed moving on my side. John suspected I had gotten off early from the diner, saw him there thinking he was asleep, and came in to lay down. After a few minutes, he said he turned over to say something to me, only to find that no one was there.

He went on to say that he had a lot of different things happen when I wasn't there. I respected that he didn't want to talk about these things, but it would have certainly helped to confirm I wasn't going insane if he would have told me. After he finished speaking, our pastor reiterated his opinion that we should move out of the house. He and his wife simply didn't grasp the fact that we have every last cent to our names tied up in that house.

I understood that the state of our souls was more important, but there most certainly had to be a way that we could resolve things by some other means than hitting the road. Especially after particularly frightening events, it was ever-present in my mind that we might have to walk off and leave everything like the previous owners, but I prayed that day would never come. There had to be some way to get rid of the malicious forces that made its home in ours. "If there is," I thought, "I need to find it before it's too late." I knew that there was something that had happened in the house or on that land that could be undone to stop all of the activity that plagued us. I yearned for the time that saw the end of me praying each night that we would live to see the light of day once more.

26

A few weeks after the blessing, my granddaughter Rachel came to stay with us. It was the first time since her ordeal that happened. Rachel and I were in the living room watching cartoons and playing beauty shop when we heard what sounded like a loud gunshot. At first, everything went out in the house for a few seconds, then came right back on. A couple of fleeting seconds later, we heard the noise again. This time, it sounded as though it were coming from within the house.

I decided to go outside and look around, and then check everything inside as well. After being outside for a few seconds, I started to turn and go back in the house. It was then that I noticed a flame about a foot tall creeping down one of the wires leading to the house. I was initially more mesmerized than frightened.

Snapping to, I realized that once the flame got to the house, it would catch fire. I ran into the house and called 911. When the fire chief got there, he saw the flame dancing on the wire and appeared to be in disbelief of what he was seeing. He asked what we had in the house. Confused, I told him nothing more than anyone else who had lived there. I invited him to look around if he didn't believe me. He remarked that he had never seen a flame that tall on a wire before.

I began to question in my mind whether the demon could have had anything to do with this. I was also curious as to just how a flame could have started in the middle of a wire like that anyhow. From there, I found my mind playing back the way Daisy would always whisper after being here so, "he wouldn't hear us." I also thought of the time when my husband had called home and Rachel answered. I remember clearly as she brought the phone to me how she was carrying the phone by her side, swinging it back and forth until she handed it over.

I took the phone and said, "hello." John asked, who was on the line while Rachel was taking me the phone. "No one." I told him. He told me that the whole time until I said "hello," all he could hear was growling on the phone. I wonder now if what's in the house can listen to us, even when we're on the phone. Was whatever this thing was trying to burn the wire in two so we couldn't call out, or perhaps call for help if we needed it? Maybe it simply was trying to burn the house down around us. I hoped to find out before it was too late.

27

We try to spend a fairly equal amount of time with our grand-kids, and it was time for my grandson Steven to come and stay the night with us. Steven absolutely loves to play games on his game console, so I imagined that would be a good portion of our weekend. He is the only one of his siblings that has asthma, and he keeps his inhaler in his pocket at all times.

After going to bed on his first night over, Steven woke up at some point during the night. He had been sleeping on a pallet he made up on the floor next to our bed. He woke me up and I asked him if everything was alright.

"I keep hearing knocking." He said. "And every time I set my inhaler down, something keeps moving it."

"Do you think you could just be hitting it in your sleep?" I asked him, trying to play it off and keep him from worrying.

He shook his head. "No Nan. I've been hit in the head twice by it. It's like someone is throwing it just to hit me. After the first time, I had it in my pocket. I don't know how it got back out or who's throwing it. I came in here when it all started and made my pallet, hoping it would stop, but it hasn't. I don't know what's going on."

I told him I would hold on to it, and promised it wouldn't happen again. As he handed it to me, I was hoping I could keep that promise.

28

I usually slept with the TV on, but for some reason, I decided to leave it off one night. I couldn't sleep, so I was just laying in bed, looking around. I directed my attention to the ceiling at a huge light that seemingly appeared out of nowhere. It was as large as a ceiling fan and shaped like a puzzle piece. At first, I started to get up and run out of the room. I was so afraid, I felt like my heart was going to beat out of my chest.

Realizing it was between me and the doorway, I sat up in the bed and watched this mysterious light. It appeared thick and yellowish in color. I never took my eyes off of it, afraid of what might be next. I tried to wake my husband, but it seemed that I couldn't get him to wake up. I began to worry that the house may be on fire, but there was no smoke or anything else that would indicate that. I noticed different colors running through the light.

It all lasted for maybe a minute at most. I thought it would go through the ceiling or the wall, but it didn't. It appeared to close like a door. Just before the door closed, what appeared to be a thick, puffy shadow dropped down out of the light, went out of my bedroom door, and down the hall. I thought about this peculiar event as I stayed in bed, not sure of what to do next.

I was curious as to where the shadow went. Was the light an actual gateway to the other side? To think that something that had dropped out of this door was now roaming around my house sent chills down my spine. I firmly believed that everything that was in the house wanted me to know beyond a shadow of a doubt, it was back. The eerie feeling came over me that the house was truly theirs and we were only visiting. Furthermore, I couldn't shake the feeling that something evil once took place here. If I hadn't experienced everything that had happened to that point, I would not have believed it. I felt that we were living in a horror movie that kept looping back, playing out without end.

It had been a month or so since I had seen the light in my bedroom. The knocking can be heard almost every night without fail. One night in particular, I woke up at some point, without any immediately apparent cause. When I opened up my eyes, I could see that the ceiling was faintly lit, and I could see something crawling across the ceiling. It vaguely resembled a gigantic spider. Whatever it was made its way across the ceiling until it finally passed through the wall on my husband's side of the room. Even against the darkness of the room, I could see what appeared to be deep black legs coming out of this "spider."

When we got up that next morning, I noticed scratch marks on John. It looked as if someone with thin finger nails had raked them down his back. Looking back, I had noticed having scratches on myself in the past, but thought nothing of them until that moment. I also thought about times when scratches appeared on my grand-kids. In those cases, I thought what other adults would likely think: they had got them while playing outside.

One time in particular, involving my grandchildren, comes to mind. One night, my grandson, Nick, came to stay with us. The evening was largely unremarkable, nothing serious occurred and we all had a fun time. The next morning, however, I saw three large scratches running down his chest. I asked him what happened, but he told me he didn't know. I certainly had my suspicions, but in order not to scare him, I said nothing.

Another night, Nick came to stay with us again. It was always nice to have the kids around, as they had a way of bringing light and life into the house. At that time, Nick, who was six, loved Spider-Man. He had brought with him his Spider-Man blanket, the most recent movie that had come out, and his Spider-Man PJ's. That night as we laid on the couch, we must have watched that movie at least three times. Finally, I peaked at Nick, who was covered head-to-toe with his blanket, and seen he was fast asleep. Thinking he would be fine there, I let him sleep there instead of carrying him to bed. I left a light on for him, just in case, and went to bed.

Around six the next morning, I pried myself out of bed. Usually I'm up earlier, but staying up late and repeatedly watching *Spider-Man* has a way of taking it out of you. I went to the door of the living room thinking I would find Nick still asleep. To my surprise, I found him laying on the couch, eyes wide open, and staring at the ceiling. As if this wasn't odd enough, his arms and legs were straight out. I called his name several times before he ever answered.

He told me that he hadn't been able to move all night. "When I woke up, you were gone, and I couldn't move my arms or my legs." He said. "The only thing I could move were my eyes, and I could see these bright lights all around me. I wasn't scared, but I didn't like that I couldn't move. What's wrong with me Nannie?"

Again, I had my thoughts, but kept them to myself. I walked over and put my arms around him to calm and reassure him. At that point, I was needing someone to do the same for me.

Having sat with him a bit, I got him up off the couch and we had breakfast. As we ate, he was talking all about Spider-Man, and wanted to know if we could watch the movie one more time before he had to leave. I was glad that he was seemingly able to moved so quickly past what had happened. I told him we could, but only after he got cleaned up and got dressed.

As I ran his bath water, Nick was getting undressed, and it was then that I noticed the thick scratches on his neck. They weren't like the ones before. These ran from his neck down to his chest. Again, I asked how he got them, and again, he said he didn't know. All he knew was that they were there when he woke up and they felt like they were burning.

When my daughter came to pick him up, she saw the marks on his neck. Naturally, she had a fit. Like myself, she wanted to know why the house blessing didn't seem to have worked.

"Mom, you've got to be kidding." She said quietly, so as to not be over heard. "I can't let my kids go through this. Have you took a good look at Nick's neck? You've got something in this house that must be pure evil to do that to a child."

She was right of course. Whatever was in this house wasn't good at all, and to make matters worse, the house blessing was ineffective to say the least. After this, Sherry and her husband were sitting with me at the kitchen table discussing what happened with Nick. My husband, wondering what all the fuss was about, came into the room and sat down. As we started to tell him, the lights above the table began to flicker on and off. Everyone went silent. As we watched the light, the picture above the kitchen window, a good fifteen feet away, flew off the wall and landed at John's feet.

In a state of disbelief, my daughter jumped up and exclaimed, "No way!" Not hesitating, they picked up Nick and made a b-line for the door. My son-in-law, as he bolted from the house, swore he would never step foot in that house again. I wanted to try to convince them to stay, but I couldn't do it; especially when I would have loved to run too, if I could have. Still unsteady from everything that had just happened, I picked up the picture and uneasily hung it up, half expecting it fly right back off. I read the words written on the picture and couldn't help but to find it a little funny: "Good morning: let the stress begin!"

30

If it weren't for others experiencing things here as well, I would think that I was going crazy, just like the doctor had. I was able to get my hands on a copy of the deed to the house, after a fair amount of searching. Looking over the names of the previous owners, I was able to recognize some, but others, I had no clue as to who they were. Wanting to reach out to any of them that would talk to me, I began to cross-check the names on the deed with the phone book. "Certainly, a few must still live in this area." I had thought. As it turned out though, most all of them were dead or had moved far away.

Not long after finding the deed, I was at the diner working when I got a surprise. Much to my disbelief, one of the former owners walked through the door, whom I hadn't seen in years. Fate had seemingly intervened. The last I had heard, he and his wife had gotten a divorce while living at the house on Beech Grove. Divorce would prove to be a reoccurring trend for couples who lived there.

While pouring his coffee, I asked, "Are you Jeff Jones?"

He looked at me for a moment and asked with a light tone, "Who want's to know?"

I told him who I was and asked if he would be alright with talking about the house where he used to live. He cracked a slight smile as if he knew exactly what I was wanting to know about. As I sat down at the table with Jeff, I asked if he had ever heard or saw anything unusual while staying there.

Gazing off into his memories, he began to speak. "I've got two boys. They lived with me there after my wife and I got divorced. They would complain that they heard knocking at night and saw shadows in different parts of the house. I, of course, told them it was nothing. One night, I found myself being woke up by the same knocking. Curious as to what it was and where it was coming from, I got up out of bed and went through the house checking the doors."

"Even though I didn't find anything, I still felt scared; the likes of which I hadn't felt since I was a child. That night, I did something that I had never done before or since: I went to bed with a shotgun gripped tight in my hands. As crazy as it might sound, there was some unseen danger in the house that night. I laid awake until morning light, not knowing what might happen next. Not long after, I sold the house."

I asked if he had ever seen anything outside the house. "There was one time." He said while closing his eyes. "Early one morning, before the cool mist in the air had lifted, I do remember seeing something in the woods. First, I seen movement in one area, but the longer I looked, others began to appear. Finally, there was a half dozen, of what looked like people in costumes from different times, walking in the woods."

"All I could do was watch in silence at first, as they seemed to glide silently around. I thought someone might be playing a trick on me, that was until I could have swore I seen right through one of the people. At that moment, I was so scared I thought I might get sick. Mustering up my courage, I did manage to call out to the figures, but there was no reply."

"After what seemed to be a couple of minutes, all of the figures vanished without a trace. Cautiously, I made my way out to where I had seen some of them. I found nothing. There were no footprints, no sign of anyone running away through the woods, absolutely nothing. And honestly, I was glad there wasn't."

Far from comforted, I thanked him for his time. I wanted to ask him more about everything that had happened, but I had to get back to work. While somewhat skeptical, I still wondered who the figures could have been. Certainly, there couldn't have been that many people die on our property. Where could they have all come from? Typical of what I had found to that point, I was left with more questions than answers.

32

In a small town, word gets around fast when you start asking questions about people. Today, I had a preacher that lives just down the road from us come by the diner and tell me to stop by after I got off. When I asked why, he told me that he wanted to talk to me about a couple that had lived in the house a while back. On my way home that day, I saw him working in his yard and remembered what he said. Pulling into his driveway, I asked him what information he had to share about the couple and the house.

He told me that the couple was divorced now, but when they lived there, he and the husband, whose name was Chad, had gotten to be good friends. The man knew my neighbor was a preacher and asked him for "help with his wife." As he told it, he was worried about the things she was doing in the house. It turned out that

Chad had bought the old upright piano for his wife, because she wanted to learn how to play. He proceeded to hire a piano teacher to teach her, only for the piano teacher and wife to end up having an affair, as he would later find out.

Hurt over the affair, he told my neighbor that he was still worried about his wife. He said that she would go into one of the bedrooms at night, draw a pentagram on the floor, light candles, and chant. After some time, his wife left him for the piano teacher and joined the cult that the teacher belonged to.

Amazed at what I was hearing, I asked what happened to the husband and where he was now. My neighbor told me that Chad had moved to Illinois and that they still talked from time to time. As of late, he said, Chad had begun to slip mentally. It seemed that the whole ordeal with his wife proved too much for him. It had gotten so bad, in fact, that he moved in with his father, who ended up dying not too long after. His dad left him well off and in want for nothing, but in his current state of mind, he wasn't able to enjoy life, with or without money.

I was pleased to have finally found out the story behind the piano. As grateful I was for the information, I wondered what else I would find out about my house. In hopes for more concrete evidence, I went to the courthouse and public library to see what I could dig up. Despite my efforts, and that of the staff, I didn't find anything of any real help. Thus far, most everything I found out was by word of mouth, as I have shown. I started to wonder if the house would ever give up its secrets.

33

Some time after, I woke up one night to the smell of sulfur. I had never smelt that before anywhere in the house that I can recollect. Feeling that there was also something in my room, I was too afraid to open my eyes, so I kept them tightly shut. It was like I could feel something right in front of my face, pungent with the smell of sulfur, and trying to suck the breath from my body. I always sleep on my side, facing away from my husband, but when I felt this, I turned quickly to face him. I kept my eyes closed out of fear.

From the darkness, the strangest thing: I felt as though there was something else in the room. It was as though I could sense the spirit of a child that was hiding from this evil presence. I would like to explain more about this, but I don't know how. The best I can say is that it was as if I could share in the fear that the child was feeling.

34

Following the events of that night, I had to wonder if any of the couples that had lived there, besides Jeff, had a child/children while there. If so, perhaps one of them had lost a child while living there. More than anything, I couldn't get over the feeling of a frightened child spirit being in my bedroom, hiding out of fear of some evil entity. I even began to wonder if whatever was trying to take the breath from me was also holding the child hostage somehow.

Naturally, I began to think of my little grandchildren and fear for their safety and well being. I only knew of one other person who had been in the house by name, and that was the former doctor. How I was going to find out anything useful about this child was beyond me. I was slightly reassured by the fact that the more I dug into the house and property, the more people were talking about what they knew. I came to the conclusion that I would have to wait and hope for the best.

My husband asked, "Even if you find out other children have lived here, how will you know the right one?" Uncertain, I told him, "I'll just know." Deep inside, I felt that the spirit I had sensed was a little boy around nine or ten years old.

I wasn't sure if there had been anything on the property before the house, but I do know that it was built in 1964. They had cut down a good chunk of the hill it now sits on and positioned the house feet away from a pond that was already there. One of the first names documented after the building of the house was the Dubois family. Whether or not they built the house, I don't know.

It would be a whole lot easier if everyone connected with the house wasn't dead, scattered to the four winds, or insane.

35

One day, my grandchildren and I decided we would take a walk through the woods together. We thought it would be nice to get out and get some fresh air. Aimlessly, we wandered up behind the house and around the near-by pond. As we made our way around, one of the kids called out for me to come look at a couple of the trees. Making my way over, I asked what they found, and they told me that there was 'writing' on the trees.

I could tell by looking at the carvings that they had been there for years. There was moss growing in the scars. I took a stick to clear the moss from the lettering until I could read what was there. One of them read: "Dillon drowned." The other one read: "Dillon drowned 1964 – Dillon Dubois." As I stood back reading this, I wondered if this was the child spirit I had felt in my bedroom. Did he want me to find the carving? If he did: why?

36

After finding the carvings, I was glad to at least have a name. I started to research once again, but this time, looking for information on the boy. Word got around town I was looking for information, and before long, a man I went to school with called me up at the house. He told me that Dillon was a boy that went to our school. I didn't recollect that at all. He went on, saying that Dillon had rode our school bus and that his family hadn't lived here very long before, one day, he stopped going to school. We never heard anything about him and no one seemed to talk about him, until one day our teacher told us that Dillon had "drowned in a pond near his house." He told me that the main reason he remembered Dillon so well, was that where normally if a kid died, it would be all over town, but in his case, it was like nobody said anything. Only days after he died, the family packed up and left, leaving the house vacant for some time.

37

My oldest grandson Joseph was in the school band and decided he wanted to play the drums. Wanting to encourage him, John and I went and bought him a nice second-hand set for him to practice with. He had been staying with us quite-a-bit around that time, as his parents were getting a divorce. Poor boy had been having trouble with that, as I imagine the other kids had been too. Being fourteen then, we thought we could offer him some escape from all of that by coming to stay with us.

The day that his mom came to pick him up, he said he would rather stay with us until the divorce was over. I felt sorry for Sherry, not only was she loosing her high-school sweetheart, now her son didn't even want to go home. I left her and Joe to talk, they had always been close, but I knew that at the end of the day she would give in to his wishes without letting him forget how much she loved him. He could have went home anytime he wanted, but I knew that he wasn't going to be holding his breath for it.

38

Joseph moved in, taking what used to be Sarah's bedroom that is right across from our own. Sarah left home as soon as she got out of high school. She thought she was in love. She let us know that she was eighteen and didn't want to live in a haunted house anymore. I didn't blame her as far as that went. The man she left with was twice her age, which set our teeth on edge. Powerless to stop her, and as she seemed happy, we wished her the best and let her know she always had a home.

I still believe that things would have been different were it not for the house. Sarah had always been a pretty tame child, but after moving into the house on Beech Grove, that seemed to change a little at a time. True, she was also going through the teenage years and all that, but there seemed to be something more. We used to go to church every Sunday as a family, but over time, Sarah stopped wanting to go. All she did want to do was hang out in the basement with her friends.

One Sunday night, I talked Sarah into going to church with us. That night was supposed to be a special one, as a prophet of our faith was set to guest preach. Half-way through the sermon, Sarah looked over at me and said, "Do you really believe in this?" "Don't you?" I asked. She never said if she did or not.

At the end of the sermon, the prophet asked if anyone wanted to be prayed for. To my great surprise, Sarah wanted to go up front and have him pray for her. Looking like she was scared to death, she asked me if I would go with her. About half of the church had gone up. When the prophet, who didn't know us from Adam, got to Sarah, he put his hand on her forehead and said, "Come out, demon!"

Immediately, Sarah fell to the floor; her whole body shaking violently. In disbelief, I watched as her body appeared to lift off the floor about two or three inches. I looked to our pastor's wife, whose eyes were as big as saucers, looking for an explanation for what was happening. She told me to wait while the pastor and another man carried her to the pastor's office. There was a small group of people including our pastor's wife that was back there for quite some time, praying over Sarah.

Once they were finished, all of them looked like they had been through the ringer. They all reassured me that everything was going to be alright. I was told that something evil had taken hold of Sarah, and that was what they were praying to liberate her from. On the way home, I asked Sarah if she believed it was real now. Exhausted, she nodded her head, "It's real."

I truly believe that Sarah had been possessed, and not just because someone else said so either. Later on, I found out that she and her friends had been playing with an Ouija board down in the basement. After she left home, she confessed that was what they were doing down there. I didn't want to imagine what doors they might have opened.

The thought of them down there playing around like that brought me back to when we moved in. While bringing in our things, I saw where it looked like someone had built a small fire in the middle of the basement floor. A little while after, I found a book on witchcraft on one of the shelves down there that hadn't been there when we looked at the house previously. Not knowing what else to do, my husband took the book outside and burned it. Also, concerned that someone might have broken in though the basement door to perform some ritual, he sealed the door that leads out from the basement shut: just as it remains to this day.

39

After Sarah left home, the basement was empty once again. Joseph thought that it would be great to have his drum set down there, so that's where we moved it to. The next morning, while standing at the kitchen sink, I heard one of the drums play. It was a deep sound that lead me to believe it came from the bass drum. Looking at the kitchen clock, I saw that it was just a little past eight: too early for playing drums. I opened the basement door and seen that the lights were off. I went down the hallway heading to Joe's room, ex-pecting to find his bed empty. To my surprise, he was sound asleep.

A little later on, I told my husband about hearing the drums playing. His theory was that a mouse had hit the drum, and that's what caused the noise. I was skeptical of this, however. Thinking to myself, "In order for me to hear that drum upstairs and with the door closed, his name would have had to have been 'Mickey!'" Bang went that theory.

Never-the-less, I decided to go down into the basement to see if maybe we did have a mouse problem. As I headed for the basement door, I can remember thinking I would much rather it had been anything else, as I can't stand mice or bugs. I reached to turn on the lights but, once again, it didn't work. Grabbing a nearby flashlight and a new light bulb, I swapped out the old bulb and tried the switch again: nothing.

Not deterred, I gripped my flashlight, and waded into the darkness. I looked around for a few minutes, finding nothing out of the ordinary. As I was about halfway back up the steps, flashlight still shinning bright, I frozen in my tracks. Between the steps, peered two piercing red eyes, veiled in the darkness of a distant corner.

I flicked the light over to the corner, but the eyes didn't move. Huge and unwavering, they continued to watch as if stalking prey. Not waiting for the predator's pounce, I flew up the stairs, slamming the door behind me. Eyes on the door, not knowing what would happen next, I backed my way into a kitchen chair and sat down to catch my breath. My body still, my mind kept racing as I tried to reason away what I had just seen. Unable to come up with any logical solution, I continued to sit there and watch the door, my mind searching the darkness just behind.

About that time, John came walking in through the back door to retrieve his billfold. No sooner had he stepped inside, that I told him about the eyes in the basement. He took the flashlight from me and went to the basement. Though I had told him about the lights, he instinctively hit the switch: the lights flickered to life. I looked on, more confused then than ever. I know I tried those lights and they didn't work. When he came back upstairs, he assured me that the basement was sealed tight and there was no way that anything could get down there.

We sat and talked some more about what happened. While we were talking, Sherry walked in. I proceeded to fill her in on everything that was going on. Having heard that morning's excitement, she came up with the idea of the three of us taking our camcorder and, after dark, video taping our way through the house to see if we could capture anything on film. I wasn't sure about her plan. Mainly, I wasn't sure that my daughter, who is scared of her own shadow, was going to actually go through with this hair-raising little plan.

I went about my business that day in anticipation for the evening that would follow. I began thinking about some of the stories I had heard when I was a child about the small town we lived in. I used to sit and listen to the old folks talk about how wild our sleepy little town used to be. Now the county is dry, no alcohol, but even as close as in my parents day, there were bars, dance halls, shootings, hangings, and all manner of excitement going on.

To boot, there are ancient Native American burial mounds about a mile away from the house we live in now. Until recently, they had the bones of many people, including children, on display to the public. While the bones have been re-interred, the rest of the site remains open to this day. We also sit on part of the Lewis and Clark trail. Just a stumble away, is the convergence of the Mississippi and Ohio Rivers. Here three states come together: Missouri, Illinois, and Kentucky.

Across from our town is the city of Cairo, Illinois, which was a part of the Underground Railroad. This made me think of the old plantation house that had been built by slaves for my great-great-great-grandmother. Her husband had the house built while she went on a trip further down south. While not as grandiose as some of the plantation houses further south, it was still a fine house. I had visited the house once when I was younger. I remember as I ran my hand over the bricks, I was struck by the thought that each one was laid by a slave.

Thinking about all of the brutality, pain, and bloodshed that had gone on in a five square mile area: what would we find or hear? This of course doesn't even include the history of the forts and other events that have taken place here. Then I thought about the recording I had captured of "Prisoner 910." He had a to be a prisoner in the Civil War. There were, and still are, no prisons near by. I was really apprehensive about what we might find or stir up as we played ghost detectives.

Regardless of my concerns, Sherry was determined to get to the bottom of what was going on in our home. She was tired of having to worry about her children coming over to our house, and tired of them being afraid. After the kids and I had found the carvings about Dillon on the trees, and learned about him drowning, and then thinking about Daisy drowning, she was not about to take any chances. I remember her pressing us to get rid of the swimming pool, just-in-case. She argued that with everything going on around the house, that anything was possible. I found myself having a hard time trying to refute her point.

"I don't want any of the kids to be out at the pool by themselves." She said sternly. "I don't think I'll be taking them fishing over at the pond anymore either. You remember what happened to Uncle Charles last year and how his boat flipped over while he was out in the middle? If he didn't know how to swim or if he'd got tangled up, he wouldn't have made it out. No one even knew he was over there until after-the-fact. As sick as he is with COPD, he's lucky he didn't end up sick to death."

40

Sherry arrived at the house that night just as it was getting dark. It seemed the time had finally come. My husband and I were on the front porch when she got there. I had the camcorder ready. I was really surprised that she was actually going to go through with this. I imagine there's nothing we wouldn't do for our children.

"Y'all ready?" she asked. I laughed a bit at how determined she was to do this. I gave the camcorder to John so he could take care of the videotaping. I followed in behind him with Sherry clutching my shirt from behind. We kept the house dark as we went through; the camera was the only light by which we could navigate.

The entire time we were recording upstairs, we could hear noise coming from the basement. It seemed that whatever was in the house was trying to tell us that they were down there and we were in the wrong place. As we started down the basement steps I could feel Sherry tighten her grip on the back of my shirt. It seemed that some of her "gung-ho" had gone home. I knew she was afraid of what we might find in the basement, not that I blamed her.

After stepping off the last step into the basement, it felt immediately as if someone had their hands on either side of my head and was squeezing them together with all of their might. I kept rubbing my head, trying to get some relief from the pressure, but without any effect. About that time, John told us to look at the camcorder screen. As we all scrunched up around him to look at what he was seeing, we noticed a round light, about the size of a basketball, by the back wall of the basement.

I asked John if the light could be coming from the video camera itself, so he reached up and turned the camera light off. To our dismay, the bright orb continued to shine. We could only see the light through the camera and not with our bare eyes. While we questioned what the light might be and where it was coming from, we began to hear the sound of things being thrown around in the basement. The noise stopped as suddenly as it started. Frightened, we looked around to find an origin or cause, but found nothing.

Going back to where we were previously, we found the light was still hovering there where we had left it. Was the same thing causing the light also causing the noises? To me, it seemed that whatever was throwing things was behaving like a creature that had been cornered and wanted to let us know that we weren't welcome. I considered that the noises were a distraction to keep our attention away from someone or something unseen. It made sense to me, as in my experience, having objects thrown at you isn't an invitation to come closer or stick around.

Finally, Sherry said she had had enough and was going to go upstairs and turn the lights on. Once I had got back up stairs, the pressure that I had felt in my head left. We sat together as we reviewed the tape. Each of us were amazed at the orb that we had seen in the basement. As we went around to capture other parts of the basement on video, the orb stayed against the back wall. No other lights were on, and no light could come in from the outside that would have been able to explain it. Furthermore, there were no other living beings down there except for us that could have thrown things around and made noises like we heard.

The best was yet to come though. At the end of the recording, just as we were heading back up, we unknowingly captured one last piece of evidence. In the last bone-chilling seconds, we could hear a voice. It wasn't benign like "Prisoner 910" had been, this voice sounded evil. We listened carefully and could make out the voice saying: "Get out. You don't belong here."

At hearing the voice, a collective chill ran through the room. It was well inferred before, but now it was explicitly clear: something really did not want us here. We discussed among ourselves as to whether we should go back down or not. Sherry was against it more than anyone. I didn't feel like pushing it much either. As with other discoveries I had made about that place, I was left with more questions than answers. Would I ever get to the bottom of it all? Would this home ever be fully ours?

41

When I began to keep a diary, I wanted to keep it about what was happening at the house, but it would seem that there is more at play than what is going on here. One day after our little "ghost hunt," was an incident I have to write about; though I am almost to petrified to do so. My grandson Joseph and I both experienced this, but I am certain that people would still think we were crazy if we told them. If it hadn't been for Joe being with me and seeing the same thing I did, I wouldn't have believed it myself.

We were out driving and on our way towards the local paper mill just outside of town. It was right around dusk, and we had just passed the cross where Daisy had committed suicide and were going down the back side of Fort Jefferson Hill. Right in that area, there was a small patch of woods on the passenger side, just around the curve from the cross. Being fairly light still, I didn't even have my headlights on yet as we went along.

As we passed this spot, I had just glanced over towards Joseph and the woods. It was only a second, but just enough time to make eye contact with something standing in the woods. Unable to believe my eyes, I took a quick double take over my shoulder as we passed. Real or not, there was no way on earth I was going to stop or go back to check if what I saw had really been there.

Little to my knowledge at that time, Joe had also seen the figure. As I rounded the curve and checked my mirrors again, I loudly asked, "What in the world was that?!" I looked over at my grandson who looked as if he had seen a ghost. Stunned, he asked if I had seen it too. Not wanting to bias his answer, I asked him what exactly he thought he had seen. This way, I figured I would really be able to know for sure that we both had seen whatever it was that had been there.

With a tone of mixed fear and excitement in his voice, he asked: "Nannie, have you ever seen that movie *Jeeper's Creepers*? That's the only way I can describe what I just saw."

I don't think either of us would have seen that thing if I hadn't been going around the curve so slow. He was right though, whatever it was, it looked just like the bad guy from the movie, or some kind of winged demon. It was unlike anything I had ever seen before. It stood between two trees, as if waiting for us to pass. The creature looked to be eight or nine feet tall at least. I can still see its huge, pitch black eyes as they met mine. What looked like two tremendous wings covered its body until the moment our eyes made contact. It was at that moment, it appeared to fly straight up without a movement. I don't know where it went, but I do know that Joseph and I had seen the same terrible image.

42

I remember one night, waking up to my husband feeling around the bed. At first, I thought that he couldn't sleep and was trying to find the remote control so he could watch TV. I finally grabbed the remote and handed it to him before drifting back off to sleep. The next morning, after we had been up a little while, he started to talk about that previous night.

"Nancy," he started, looking very serious. "I want you to tell me the truth: were you serious or just kidding around last night?"

"What are you talking about?"

He said, "Last night, I woke up to what I thought was you laying up against my back whispering things in my ear. When I rolled over to face you, you had your back towards me. When you woke up and felt me feeling the bed, I wasn't looking for the remote, I was trying to establish how close you were to me."

"It wasn't me. Maybe you've got a ghostly girlfriend." I joked. He didn't even crack a smile. Whatever it was genuinely spooked him. To my knowledge, this was the first time anything like this had happened to either of us: would it be the last?

43

I had gone to spend the day with my mother. I hadn't been to see her in a while, so it was an overdue visit. I thought it would be good for both of us to spend some time together and get away from our problems for a little while. Right before I was about to walk out the door, the phone rang. I heard my mother say, "Oh my God! Not again!"

My heart sank and I braced for what might follow. As I started towards her to ask her what was going on, she handed the phone over to me and went to sit down. She looked absolutely shattered. I put the phone to my ear to hear the news: my oldest brother, Greg, had committed suicide. I was shocked to say the least. I couldn't believe that he would do such a thing, especially after Daisy's death and seeing how if affected everyone in the family. I remember that he had stayed with us for a few days and he was so upset that Daisy would kill herself. Now, after everything, he had done the same thing. I just couldn't bring myself to believe it.

Unlike Daisy, he chose a bullet to be his means to an end. His suicide note, however, read almost identically to Daisy's. He wrote that he was in a terrible amount of pain, though from what, I don't know. I weakly made my way to the dinner table and had a seat with my mother. Sitting there I thought how my oldest brother and sister had taken their own lives. Would there be any more of my siblings do the same thing?

I began to worry about myself, as I had started to hurt in my back and legs. One time, I remember thinking that if Daisy hurt any worse than I was, I could almost understand why she did what she did. It seemed like the whole family was falling apart. It was like there was some kind of curse on us. We used to be a family that was very tight knit and happy. Since Daisy died though, it seemed like we were all living in our own little worlds. Each of us were inundated with out own family issues and it was nearly impossible to keep up with one another as we used to. Thankfully, my sister Ruth and I remain close, and I ask her advice about practically everything. I don't know what I would do if anything happened to her.

44

Sometime after this, I was laying in bed late one evening, watching TV. As I laid there, I seen a thick black mist hanging over my bed. At the same time I was staring at this mist, my grandson Joseph came out of his room on his cellphone. I started to call out to him as he walked on down the hallway. The black mist wouldn't get away from me, even as I waved my hands in front of my face trying to bat it away and make it leave.

It seemed like it was trying to get me out of bed. As I was about to oblige and get up, Joe came into the bedroom saying that he had some bad news. I sat up as he told me a friend I had worked with for years had died. Had that been the cause of the mist I had seen, or was something trying to warn me perhaps? That was the first time I had ever seen a mist. Prior to this incident, I had always seen dark shadows instead. I wonder what the difference, if any, could be.

45

For the first time in months, we had some guests come over for supper. We had just finished building the deck in the back yard, just for such occasions. John and I both missed having cook-outs with friends and family, and generally living a normal life. I had recently been to the mall to by a new CD by a well-known family gospel group to share with my sister-in-law, Phyllis.

Phyllis and her husband arrived and we all sat out and ate and talked, and generally forgot about life's problems for a while. It was great to have them over and enjoy their company. After a while, Phyllis and I left the fellas on the deck and we went in to listen to my new CD. Unfortunately, the only means of playing it was Sarah's old stereo that she had left downstairs. Thinking it would be fine, I took her down to the basement.

As the second song began to play, a candle we had burning on the table flew off and hung in midair for what seemed to be forever. We both watched in amazement as the candle finally hit the floor. Phyllis, eyes wide, turned to me and said, "Did you see that?" Of course I had. We both grabbed our drinks and hurried upstairs.

Phyllis said she couldn't believe what she had just seen. "That candle just hung in midair like someone was holding it. I don't think y'all are living here alone."

We had originally planned for her to spend the night, as we were all supposed to head down to Tennessee the next morning and visit a couple of sites that we had been longing to see. She voiced some concern at first, but after talking to her a bit, she agreed to stay. We had told her about the house, but like most people, she didn't believe us until she saw it for herself.

46

Come the next morning, I was glad that nothing serious happened during the night. I heard Phyllis, or what I assumed and hoped was her, get up a few times over the course of the night. I asked her how she had slept. It was then she told me that during the night, she had got up to go to the bathroom and have a drink of water.

When she reached the kitchen, she said that all of the cabinet doors were open and all of the drawers were pulled out. I didn't want to tell her that this was something that happened almost every night here. After a while of living in a haunted house, I guess you can get used to certain things that would have rattled you pretty good previously. At that point, I would go around and shut everything and go on about my business. What else could I do? Later on, as we were heading out, she laughed a little and asked if they could cook too. "If only," I thought. "And if they would clean too, I wouldn't be so eager to be rid of them." All kidding aside, the activity in the house was steadily getting worse. Not so much getting darker, but getting more frequent.

47

We were gone all that weekend. We felt better, we weren't tired at all the whole time we were away. I found myself wishing we didn't have to go back. I knew that once we were back in the house, our energy would be drained away and we would be right back in the struggle that I had both grown so used to, and tired of. Even so, I couldn't leave my children, grandchildren, and everything that made up my home behind. I may have dreaded the thought of going back, but I knew I had to.

In what seemed a fleeting moment of joy and rejuvenation, the weekend passed and we found ourselves back at the house. Half-way up the driveway, John stopped. "I hate the thought of even going back into that house. It won't be two hours before we'll be back to being tired and hurting and wanting to go to bed." He was right of course, though I don't think it even took two hours. While laying in bed, he remarked that what we were feeling wasn't normal and we needed to do something about it, but what, we didn't know.

We thought back to after we had just moved in and how we suspected a gas leak. John thought, perhaps the tester gave a false negative. "Yeah." I said. "But gas doesn't produce footsteps besides the bed. It also doesn't throw things, open doors, or any of the other things we've had happen here. Not to mention we would all be deathly ill or just plain dead by now. No. I'm afraid that there's no natural solution to what we have going on."

48

Not long after our return, Joseph had one of his friends from the department over for the night. They had both joined the junior fire department a few months back. They stayed in the living room playing games for hours before going to bed. A little after three in the morning, I heard Joseph's friend screaming. Running in to see what was going on, he told me that he had seen a light that was hovering over his bed.

He was scrambling around the room, frantically grabbing up his things as he was heading for the door. He ran down the hall and out the back door like an Olympic sprinter; before I could catch him, he was gone. Joe came out of his room and asked what was going on. I told him his friend said he saw a light over his bed and left. Shaking his head, Joe went back into his room, talking low under his breath. "I hate this house."

49

I had decided to have John bring the computer up from the base-ment. At first he said no. I then proceeded to inform him that was the wrong answer. I told him I was sick and tired of living like we had been, and worrying that anytime we had someone over, they were going to have an encounter with whatever demon or entity we had in this house. This place had just about taken the life out of us all, to one extent or another.

I told him about that previous Sunday, which was a perfect example. Joseph had brought his girlfriend that he met at church home to go swimming. The idea was, that she would spend the afternoon with us and we would take her back to church that eve-ning. It was nice to hear laughter around the house. I could hear them out in the pool all afternoon while I was preparing supper. Carly is such a sweet girl and talks with a quiet, southern accent. I know she'll be good for Joseph.

Supper was just about done, and it was going to be another thirty minutes before I was going to call them in from the pool.

About that time, they both came bolting through the back door, towels wrapped around them, and water still dripping off. Poor Carly looked pale as a ghost and Joseph was upset that she was upset. I could see it was all she could do to keep from crying.

I resisted the urge to tell them to stop dripping on my floor, and asked what was going on. Carly said, "There's an old woman in your bedroom!" Confused, I stared blankly back as she continued. "She was looking out your bedroom window when we were in the pool."

I was getting sick to my stomach as she went on telling me about the old woman she had seen. Anytime it came to the kids, I couldn't help but to be upset.

"I saw her face just as clear as I can see yours now. She had shoulder length black hair that looked to be oily or wet. Her face was pale and white looking. She was all wrinkled up in the face, and it looked like she was trying to tell me something, but I couldn't make out what it was. Is there someone else here?"

I hated to tell her, but I was the only one in the house. I hoped that the house didn't scare her to where she won't come back: time would tell. I really hated for this to happen to Carly, because Joseph really likes her. Later on, Joe told me, "Nannie, if we don't do something about this place, none of us are going to have any kind of a happy life." Then he asked if there was some kind of "ghost hunter" that we could call and see what they could do. "Certainly, you've seen some of the TV shows where they come to your house and get rid of whatever is in your home."

I told him that's just for TV. It makes for a good show, but that was about all it was good for. Quite convincingly, he came back with, "Maybe or maybe not, but if it is real, what do you have to lose except the entity?" I found him difficult to argue with.

Having explained everything to John, he agreed to bring the computer upstairs. I gave him a hand and we had it set up in no time. I thought that Joseph was definitely on to something with what he said. If nothing else, I would be relieved to simply know that we weren't alone in the things we were experiencing. I figured that if we weren't alone in the problem, then we wouldn't be alone in the solution.

50

The thing I was most uncomfortable with, was the thought of someone we didn't know coming into our home and stirring things up. It was bad enough having spirits swarming like hornets, the last thing we needed was someone coming in poking the nest with a stick. That was the kind of thing my mother would be interested in. She always believed in such things. The paranormal was her wheelhouse, per se.

She would often play the Ouija board at her home. Looking back, perhaps that's why my sister Ruth had been haunted when we were younger. Mama was convinced she was talking to the dead, but who knows who or what it really was. Come to think of it, she would also play that "game" with my daughter Sherry. Had I known then what I know now, I would have never allowed it. Of course, then I didn't believe in the paranormal really anyhow. It was a good story, but that was it. Who knows how many others will fall into error due to a lack of belief.

Ready to be back to a normal life, I got on the computer and typed in "paranormal activity," and a whole page came up about it online. I went into one of the pages that was on the top of the heap. I figured if they were on the top, they must be the best. I read through a few stories of people going through similar experiences as ours. I noticed most of them lived near rivers, lakes, creeks, or water of some sort. Furthermore, I noticed that many of them had been remodeling their home, just as we had done.

As I read on, there was a place at the bottom of the page where people could submit their own stories. On there, I told all about the types of things that were going on in my home. As I typed, I thought to myself that I would never hear anything back from them. Besides, their page said in bold print that they only took a few cases each year. What would be the odds they would choose ours?

51

Apparently, the odds were pretty good. To my surprise, they contacted me the very next day. They began by having one of their team call to interview me, my husband, and our grandchildren. After talking for what seemed to be two or three hours, they asked if they could possibly send out one of their team for an advanced interview in the future. I remained uneasy about having a stranger come in and poke around, but I more desperately wanted whatever that was here and not us, gone for good. I wanted us to have a safe, normal home, where we could gather without fear and be together as a family, just like it had been before.

52

One day, after making contact with the investigators, my husband was in the kitchen putting some last touches on the quarter round he had been working on. While he was working, he was hit in the back of the head with dice for one of the kids games they had stacked on the hutch. He called for me to come to him, and that's when he realized he was home alone.

He picked the dice back up and placed them back on the hutch. Spooked, he went back to what he was doing, until a few minutes later, the dice fell to the floor. He picked the dice back up and put them back where he had set them previously. He stared a moment to see if they would move, but nothing happened. Turning slowly back to the trim work, he said, "Now you leave the dice alone." Whatever was there must have listened; the dice didn't move the rest of the day.

After we went to bed, we heard a noise in the kitchen. Cautiously, we both got up and went down the hall to see what was going on. In the floor, laid the dice he had been dealing with earlier that day. It would seem that we now have a ghost that likes to play. I just hope its interest is limited to dice.

It's not that often that I sleep on the couch, but I found myself with no other recourse but to lay down. On one particular night, and on into the following day, I had a headache that went from the back of my neck on up into my eyes. I occasionally had headaches, but not quite like this. Not wanting to keep my husband up awake while trying to get rid of this pain, I figured the couch was the place to be.

By about midnight, my headache had finally eased up enough that I was able to drift off to sleep. Around three in the morning, I snapped awake, having been startled by someone who was whispering in my ear. As I opened my eyes, I could still hear a male voice talking in my right ear. I was stunned as he told me, "Get up! Go to your bedroom, it's your husband." This was all I could make out, and all I needed to.

I hurriedly got to my feet and rushed down the hall to our bedroom. As I was nearing the door, I could hear John groaning in discomfort. Rounding the corner into the room, I could see him on his feet holding both his legs. He had terrible, charlie-horse like cramps, that he was prone to get from time-to-time. Usually, I was there to help, but this time I happened to not be there, and instead, the voice woke me and let me know. Surely it wasn't coincidence.

After about an hour, the cramping stopped, and I got my husband back in bed, hoping he would get a little more sleep before having to get up and start his day. I figured that sleep wasn't going to be in my immediate future with everything that happened, so I went to make a cup of coffee. As the headache began to creep back up my neck and head, I thought about the voice that woke me. I had heard that voice before, but I couldn't put a face to the voice.

Whoever it was, I felt that they weren't trying to scare me. I was comforted that this spirit seemed to not only be friendly, but was trying to help us. That kind of spirit was one that I could put up with, even welcome. All of the others that had been trying to frighten us however, and quite effectively too, needed to go. No matter who the good spirit was, I couldn't help but to say out loud to them, "thank you."

54

The paranormal team called occasionally following our first interviews. I really wanted them to see if they could find out who "Prisoner 910" was. That had bothered me ever since I first captured it on my small recorder. The team has been asking the same questions over and over for the most part. Among the other questions they asked, they wanted to know the names of people they could talk to. The only person I could think of was the preacher that lived down our road who had been friends with the previous owner whose wife ran off with the occult practicing piano teacher.

I asked if he would talk to the team, and he said he would. He gave me his personal number that I could give to them. I later gave it to the team on one of the calls, but what came of it, I don't know. Being a tight-knit community, I had my doubts about how well they would be received. It's a small town we live in and people aren't always as inviting as they could be, at least when it came to things like this.

There were a lot of churches in this area, and most everyone around here belonged to one church or another. While they all had slightly different beliefs, they all firmly believed in the Bible. Even so, they didn't much like to talk about anything regarding the devil or demons. The way I figured it, if they believed in Christ, they had to believe in the fallen angels. After all, the Lord Himself, had expelled quite a few during his earthly ministry, and was even tempted by the devil in the wilderness. Good and bad exist, whether people like it or not.

I suppose, more than anything, people didn't like being put on the spot regarding the dark side and what they thought about it. "Perhaps," I thought, "they were suspicious that discussing such matters would bring bad things." In any case, from what I was able to find out about our sleepy little community, I wouldn't be the least surprised if the whole town was haunted in one form or another. I had a hunch that there were more skeletons hanging around than there were closets to store them in.

Who knows, really, what secrets lay hidden here. Only God knows for certain. What I know for certain is that they are here: whoever they are. Since moving into our home on Beech Grove, I have seen them, heard them, and even felt their presence beyond the shadow of a doubt. I truly believe, the evil ones at least, want our souls.

If it was just me, I would have thought, "Well, I'm just as crazy as the rest of the people that have gone off the deep end in this town." Despite being a small town, there have been quite-a-few mysterious deaths: hangings, shootings, stabbings, drownings: you name it. Just in the past ten years, there have been a noteworthy amount. No one seemed to pay attention to that though. It's something that people kept just beyond their nose, and thus, just beyond their sight. To bring it out into the open, like I was about to do, was probably going to make them think we were crazy.

I didn't care what they thought though. It was my mission from the first moment I decided to take charge of what was going on to save what family I had left. Maybe if I opened up about what was going on in my own home, people would start looking and caring about what was going on in their own homes. Perhaps they would see that there are things going on behind the veil, as it were.

55

I was hoping that the paranormal group wasn't going to take too long to come to our home. I imagined they were probably backed up with work, but all the same, I was eager for them to arrive. Next week they are supposed to have an advanced member of their team come down and scout things out. I am also anxious, because I'm certain that whatever is in the house is aware that they are coming.

56

I quickly began to notice that whenever we talked to a member of the team over the phone, the house seemed to get more active. It almost seemed like whatever was in the house was threatening us: "Bring them in and see what happens." I found myself apprehensive to bring the team in, but I knew that if we didn't do something to resolve what was going on, something was going to happen to my family. Enough had already happened to that point. I wouldn't have been able to live with myself if something happened I could have prevented.

To that point, I had lost family, seen heavy pictures and dishes thrown across the room, and almost had the house burn down like the past home we had. It had to stop, or I was confident, something terrible was going to happen. My mother was convinced, begging me even, that we should move or burn the house down. I told her not to say things like that over the phone, afraid that we would be overheard by whatever was in the house. My God! I was beginning to sound like Daisy. It was against my beliefs to call out the dead, but something had to be done. The team would have a member there in a matter of days, and who knew what would unfold from there, but it had to be better than what we had been going through.

57

For a few days, it had been pretty quite in the house. Only the usual knocking and a few shadows here and there persisted; the spirit's way of letting us know they were still with us. Thankfully, we had been able to sleep at nights with no scratches, cover pulling, or anything of the like having happened. Speaking of, I don't think I've mentioned about the covers to this point. There had been so much going on at the house, it is hard to remember it all or even capture it in writing.

At any point the covers would be pulled from us, something that used to scare us half to death, we would just pull them back up and go back to sleep. Funny how you change as time goes by.

I figured that we had simply had enough. Everyone else who had lived in the house had picked up and left; maybe these spirits didn't know how to get rid of us. I considered it might be the fact that we were a church going family.

I don't know if that could be a part or not though, as I don't know everything about the other people who were here. I did know that our church knew the battles we faced and were squarely behind us. They also knew, though they didn't make any mention of it, that the first paranormal team member would be at the house in one day. The team told us that he would be conducting one-on-one interviews and taking a first look at the house. Who knows what will follow.

58

The house never had a set rhythm. There would be times of peace only to have them be punctuated by moments of utter terror. One night, shortly before the arrival of the first paranormal member, was one of the most terrifying nights that I have ever experienced. If hell is any worse, I don't want to know. What I do know, is I have been close enough, and pray God, I will never be so near it again.

Exhausted from a long day, I collapsed into my bed, fast asleep. All of the sudden, I was woke up by the sensation of someone pulling sharply on my foot. My foot throbbing with pain, my eyes snapped open to see who it was, and what they wanted. To my horror, I saw the same horned demon as I had seen before. Cloaked in a darkness as black as sin, I could see him trying to crawl on top of me. I tried to move, to get up, to swing my fist, but nothing was happening. I laid helpless and unable to move as he continued to advance.

To my relief, I could still speak. In a desperate cry, I called on the name of Jesus Christ. A pained and tormented look crossed the fierce face of the creature atop of me. Seeing how he was affected, I asked, "In the name of Jesus Christ, what do you want?" Immediately, without the faintest sound, the evil figure vanished.

Again, I could move freely. As I was trying to come to terms with what had just occurred, I calmed down enough to feel the pain in my foot. Throwing aside the covers, I sat up and turned on the light. My foot was red from the ankle down, and small scratches could be seen. What evil had been unleashed in our home? For what crime were we subjected to this hell? I could only wait and plead that the team arrive soon and save us.

59

The day had come! The first team member was due at any time. I remembered eagerly waiting for him to drive up the hill to our home as I sat on pins and needles. Phil, the paranormal investigator, had already called and got directions to the house. I was hoping that everything went well and they would take our case.

As he drove up the hill and got out of his car, I could tell by his looks and the way he spoke that he wasn't from around here. Not that it bothered me of course, I just wanted our home back. We warmly welcomed him into our home. He started by talking about various things that we had already discussed over the phone at different times. After that, he asked us to show him around the house. He took pictures as he went through each room, studiously scanning everything as he went.

Following this, he asked if we could drive up to the cross where Daisy had committed suicide. I hadn't been up there since it happened. While driving to the cross, I mentioned to him the thing that Joseph and I had seen by the side of the road, and asked him his thoughts. I told him that we thought that it might have been the demon from the house that had followed us. I also requested that he keep that off the record, as people might be further enticed to think we were insane. He kindly seemed to agree. I wanted the team to know about it, but I was worried about the affect that it might have on my family and our home.

60

Phil stayed most of the day, and before he left, I already began to feel much better. I felt that we had finally found someone who could help us. Now all he had to do was consult with the rest of the team to see if they would take our case. There was nothing for us to do, but wait, and hope for the best. After he had left, I couldn't help but to reflect on all that had happened since our portion of the history of this house started.

With so much happening, both in our lives and in the house, I had forgotten about much, but never about what troubled me the most: Daisy. Like a thorn in my mind, the events surrounding her death would never leave. Her whispers that still echoed, her sense of fear that was still palpable, and her presence that was sorely missed, all pained me terribly. I found myself torn and tormented by questions of whether I could have helped, and what truly had driven her to take her own life.

I remember that the night after we had all went to bed, only to be rattled awake by her screams, how she said that she hadn't went to sleep, and was still mulling over everything she had left to do. Even though what she was going through was tearing her mind to pieces, she still was more concerned about her family. Always the caretaker. In Daisy's eyes, people did no wrong. They simply needed someone to love them, or help them in some way.

As I looked back, I feel that Daisy was "getting her ducks in a row." Did she think that by giving up her life, she would be saving her family from something? "I can't tell you, or he'll do something to the family." She had made that statement more than once. The questions I had then are the same as now, but now, only God knows.

61

Following our initial talks, and after receiving the first of the team members, we continued to talk back and forth by phone. Much to my relief, they decided to take our case, and the whole team would be at the house in a few days. I looked forward to all of this being over, and whatever was in the house, being gone. I could sense a normal life being just beyond the horizon, and it was a beautiful thought.

Somehow, I felt that whatever was here in my home also knew they were coming. Every time I would talk to one of the paranormal team, there would be something happen soon after. The set of drums we bought Joseph had been playing nearly every night. It was always the base drum. The set was directly under our bedroom, so we could hear it clearly: two or three beats, and then nothing. Perhaps, whoever was playing our drums, was the same that played the piano that the doctor had thrown down the steps. Steps, I might add, that were replaced by a former occupant that was a logger, who cut the lumber from land next to a Native American burial ground in Missouri. Just our luck!

62

While waiting for the day the paranormal team would arrive, the back door decided it would stop opening. No matter what we did, it seemed that the back door was trying to keep us locked inside the house. Even with the keys, it was impossible to get the door to move, short of breaking it open. We never knew, in that house, what would happen, or when.

One day, we went to town to do some shopping, leaving our oldest granddaughter, Anna, at the house. I could tell she was uncomfortable about staying alone in the house. At nineteen, Anna could pretty well take care of herself, even there. Unlike the other kids though, she has never stayed with us for any amount of time. I was sure the other kids had told her about some of the things that had went on in the house, but maybe she had found it hard to believe. After that particular day, however, she had no choice but to believe in something.

While we were shopping, we left our cellphones in the truck. A few hours had passed before we had a chance to go out and check to see if anyone had called. When we looked, there were at least ten calls from Anna. We went straight home after being unable to reach her, and she met us at the front door.

Shaking, she showed us a picture on her phone of the back door standing wide open. She told us that she didn't hear the door open, but could feel the cold air as it blew in. She came out of her room to see where the draft was coming from and found the door open. After closing it, she said it wouldn't open, just as it had been before.

Anna's mom and dad were getting a divorce: two for two regarding our kids. I tried to help look out for the kids and keep them safe, but with the things going on in the house, I wondered if I could even do that much. At any rate, I definitely think that Anna is a believer now. Not only because of what happened with the door, but because she had been woke up at night by knocking in her bedroom. She was sleeping in the same room that Daisy had been in while she was with us. Taking her phone, she had taken pictures when she has heard the noises. In one of the pictures, in one of the corners, there appeared to be a black hole of sorts in one corner. Since that time, Anna would either sleep in the living room or with her bedroom light on.

63

While cooking supper, the first of the paranormal team arrived. I was surprised when the young lady at the door introduced herself as being with the team. The rest, she told me, would be there the next day. While welcomed, it was earlier than we had expected, because they wanted to try to do some follow-up research on our property and our family. I welcomed her in and invited her to stay for supper. As it happened, two of my grandchildren were spending the night, and I was making spaghetti, so there was plenty there to feed everyone.

After we ate and I got things cleaned up, she asked if we could go around to speak with some of the neighbors. It was around eight-thirty by this time. I told her that everyone around there was probably already in bed. Thinking I was kidding with her, she kept insisting that we take a drive and see if there was anyone up and willing to talk. As we drove around, we found that every residence was dark, except one, and they didn't even come to the door.

Not surprisingly, being in the "Bible Belt" of the US, very few people would talk to them at any point in their stay. They're good people who live around our area, but I felt that mostly people didn't want to risk being called crazy or being ostracized for speaking out on an issue that seemed 'taboo.' I thought it was a shame. If for no other reason, because the team were all very nice and respectful. I was pleasantly surprised how genuinely concerned they seemed to be towards us and our situation.

64

Around ten o'clock the next day, the rest of the team arrived. I thought it would only be a few people, but to my surprise, there was a crowd of people showed up: eighteen of them by my count. It must have looked like the circus rolled into town. I could tell by the number of people, all of their equipment, and how they cared: they were there to clean house.

They put cameras in every room of the house (except the bathroom of course). I was amazed at how fast they set everything up. While preparing things in the basement, the drums played, causing them to stop for a minute or two before continuing. I think this was good for both us and them, because it showed that there was something in the house. More than this, I felt that this was a way for whatever was in the house to let them know the fun was about to begin.

The main team member spent a good amount of time talking to my husband and I. He and the rest of the team were all disappointed that the preacher down the road, as well as other interviews, had all fallen through. As I stated before though, I wasn't surprised. People here were mighty private about things. They would hardly talk to each other about dark things, even in church. This put any outsider far out of bounds, especially when they had a camera in hand. I will always find it a bit shameful, however, that people who read the Bible, go to church, and all that, will tip-toe around dealing with the devil and evil.

More than once they tried to get someone to talk to them, but it was no use. In a way, I can't blame them. I probably wouldn't have anything to do with it myself if I didn't think that this wouldn't be of help to my family. The team also tried to dig up other records and evidence from around town, but to no end. All they could do at that point was to call out whatever was in the house and confront it.

They set up huge lights outside the house that lit it up as if it were daytime. You could even see the lights from town. I knew people really didn't want anything to do with what was going on when they stopped going past the house. It wasn't long until a police officer pulled up at the bottom of the hill the house sat on and wanted to know what was going on. I almost hated to tell him the truth of what was happening. He seemed intrigued, but after asking a few questions, I could tell that he was eager to leave.

A little while after he left, someone from the local newspaper showed up. At that point, it was our turn to not talk to anyone. I didn't want a bunch of publicity, I just wanted my house back and my family to be safe. I half expected the TV news to show up next, but thankfully they didn't. Even if they did, they would have left empty handed too.

65

The first night they were all there, my husband and I stayed for dead time (3:00 a.m.). I noticed that a car had pulled up at the bottom of the hill. One of the team went down to meet the car and walk up the new arrival. I grew nervous after learning that this person was a well known medium. I decided to view this as a plus, having someone in our home who could actually talk to spirits.

As he entered our home and introduced himself, he asked that we tell him nothing about ourselves or the house. This seemed reasonable enough, but what really scared me was what he did before coming in. Just before reaching the door, he clutched his chest, as though in great pain. He backed away twice in an effort to recover before finally crossing the threshold. He then looked at my husband and told him he needed to take better care of himself.

Having turned out the lights, the paranormal team let us sit in the living room and watch the monitors with headphones on. From there, we could see and hear what the medium was doing, as well as everything else going on in the house. Not long after, John nudged me and said something had squeezed his arm. Why he didn't say anything to the team, I don't know. After all, that was what they were there for.

Right after they had started, we could see a white shadow behind the medium coming down in thin air. In the bedroom where Daisy had stayed, they had white candles burning for light. The medium asked if there was someone walking down the hallway, because he could hear footsteps. Thanks to the headphones we had on, we could hear them too.

We could also see and hear what was happening in our bedroom. There, one of the team members was sitting still and looking frightened. Over the headphones, we could hear why. I don't know if he could hear them, but we could, and he should have been scared. We were able to hear all manner of voices, though neither of us could make out what they were saying.

The candles in Daisy's room were going crazy and giving an eerie sense of life to everything. The medium said there is a woman who wants to come closer, but she's afraid, and there's someone else with her. He then asked if we knew anyone who had passed that had worked on the river for a living, had something wrong with his hand, and was missing a leg.

The other spirit, he said, was a woman who loved her family and carried her family's troubles on her shoulders, but at the time she died, she couldn't carry her own. She was afraid to enter the bedroom, because she was afraid of the spirit that was in the bedroom; the same one that spoke to her when she was alive. The medium went on to say that the spirit told the woman he would kill her.

He then asked the female spirit, whom we had identified as Daisy, to come into the room, and that her family needed her help. Again, the candles began to flicker, sending light and shadow dancing around the room. My husband and I were starting to hear the voices of men, women, and children coming through the headphones. Our blood ran cold as we looked at each other in disbelief.

Whether it was from the candles or not, John and I were amazed to see orbs in various parts of the rooms. While in awe over what we were watching, the man in our room spoke up about what he was experiencing in there. While sitting on the bed, as still as the grave, he said he was hearing knocking in one of the corners. The team turned their attention to our room at that point, but not much else happened in there.

With my mind reeling from the information we were just given, the investigation continued for a little while longer. The medium asked Daisy's spirit if she could tell who was haunting our home. One of the paranormal investigators asked if it was her who was haunting the home. The medium quickly answered, "No, but she does visit them." He also stated that Daisy told him that it was a demon in our home, more specifically, seven of them. I had figured on one, but seven . . . I felt almost nauseous at the thought.

Finally, they decided to call it a night, not that there was much left of one. The basement had to wait for the next night it seemed. Exhausted, my husband and I decided to stay in town with my mother. After arriving at my mother's, we began to talk about everything that had happened. While we went back and forth, it dawned on me who the male spirit was that was with Daisy. With our minds reeling in the moment, I hadn't connected the fact that I had a brother that had died in a car wreck some thirty-five years prior. As the medium said, he worked on the river for a living and was killed at the age of twenty. Also, just as he said, he lost his leg in the same accident.

I guess that's just the way fear works, you can't even remember basic things or events that you wouldn't be able to forget any other time. I was strangely comforted knowing that they were together. Then I thought about the footsteps, and even they made sense. My brother had always worn boots that had a distinct sound when he walked, just like what we heard over the headphones.

Given the hour, I decided to wait until we saw the team to tell them about this revelation. Feeling rather pleased with our progress, I sat and enjoyed the morning. As the morning progressed, we heard that a bad ice storm was about to come our way. We only had about twenty-four hours before it hit. Just like that, the race was on for the team to finish their work.

66

The paranormal team was already at the house by the time we arrived the next morning. We were told to keep quiet as we entered, as the medium and part of the team were already down in the basement. After a while, we were told to come down into the basement. The medium told us that by having him and the team there, we had spoiled the demon's plan. He informed us that the demon had intended on taking us all to hell.

At that point, I could feel my head being squeezed worse than it had before. Not wanting to speak the demon's name, he wrote it down for the team to read. All he would tell us, was that this demon was particular to the causing of people to fall into sexual sin. Less worrying than the demon, the medium told us that there were three springs that ran under our property, and that spirits tended to be drawn to water. For this reason, he said that we would always have spirits in our home. Following this statement, he tried to comfort us by reassuring us that not all spirits are bad. Personally, I didn't want any.

During a quick break, later that morning, I couldn't help but to think how the paranormal team treated us with such love and concern, it was like we had known them all along. My sister Ruth and her husband Will had come down to visit, I wanted her there beside me as much as possible. The paranormal team were so sweet about Ruth and mine's feelings of losing our sister to suicide.

After meeting the medium, he asked them if they had a daughter that lived in another state. Saying they did, he asked if they had a cellphone they could use to call her, so the two of them could talk. They were hesitant at first, but he quickly said that if she didn't come home soon, she would be coming home in a body bag. In shock, they called her up and handed the phone to the medium. Not saying another word to any of us, he stood up and left the room.

What they talked about exactly, he never would say. Prior to this whole experience, I would have been more dismissive, but after the previous night, I wasn't going to raise questions. Once they had finished talking, he handed the phone back. Jackie, my niece, thought that it was all a joke at first and that we had put someone up to calling. He apparently had begun by telling her exactly what he had said to her parents before the call.

Having been convinced that it wasn't a joke, she became afraid, and didn't want to talk to the medium anymore. Speaking to me, I told her more about who she had been speaking with and what was going on. I told her to take his warning seriously. She was a small town girl, living in the big city of Houston, Texas, and crime was pretty high around there. I also reminded her about the last gated community she lived in. There she had some creep that worked there that went into her apartment and stole some of her underwear. She said there was a janitor that had been watching her until the time she had enough and moved. It was all enough to make my skin crawl.

After talking a while, I felt that I had gotten through to her that this was serious and she needed to come home. I told her I loved her and hung up. The medium then turned to me and told me to remind him that he wanted to talk to me privately before he left. With everything that transpired, I forgot. That has bothered me ever since, not knowing what he wanted to discuss. Some part of me didn't want to know, but the rest of me demanded it.

Before Ruth and Will left that afternoon, the paranormal team took us up to the place where Daisy had killed herself: the cross on Fort Jefferson Hill. It was incredibly sweet of them. There, we held a small memorial for her; they even bought flowers. The tenderhearted kindness they showed truly warmed my heart.

Going into the second night, I was worried about the pending ice storm that would be on us in a few hours, on top of everything else. Earlier that day, they flew in a priest named Father Luke. He was a sizable man, and very kind. He was also an ardent believer, not only in God, but the evil that opposes God's children. Just prior to starting "dead time," Father Luke entered the house and greeted us. I supposed that whatever was in the house was already affecting him, as I could feel him trembling as I shook his hand.

As we sat in front of the monitors and got our headphones on, we saw the medium in our bedroom. He sat in a chair and had something covering his eyes. The team set up a light in front of him that drenched the whole room in red. As the priest began blessing the house, the medium seemed to slip into a sort of trance. He began mumbling, saying something we couldn't make out. Then, he shouted out the number six multiple times before mentioning the basement.

Leaving the monitors, we all headed to the basement. Going cautiously down the steps, the air seemed to have changed. Once again, I felt a squeezing in my head that I could barely stand. I began rubbing my head trying to alleviate some of the pain. Catching the eye of one of the paranormal team, he asked if I was alright. I probably should have told him, but like my husband when he felt something squeeze his arm, I didn't say anything about it.

Dead time kept crawling along with nothing dramatic happening. The medium reiterated his statement that we had three springs under the house, and this was part of the reason why spirits were drawn here. I wanted to ask him if we could put up a "do not disturb" or "no trespassing" sign to keep them away. Not thinking my humor would be appreciated, I kept my inquiry to myself.

Finally, dead time ended. The main paranormal team member told us that the "sex demon" that was in our home followed the river. He also advised us that it liked dark places, such as our basement. To help ward it off, so-to-speak, it was suggested that we fix up the basement with lights and possibly make it a game room for our grandkids. They also told us that they had sensed a little boy that stayed around the house, and that the boy had drowned in the pond near the house.

While I was processing everything, the main investigator said that the same demon we were dealing with, was invading the home of a young girl just up the river in Illinois. They were having a harder time of things than we were by the sound of it. They added that the thing that Joseph and I had seen the evening we passed the wooded area, was in fact the same demon. They held the belief that it stayed close to the river. On the lighter side, the team informed us that the spirit that was playing the old piano and our drums, was the little boy.

The team started packing up just as the storm was starting to hit. Father Luke blessed the whole house, and with his hands on top of our heads, prayed over John and I. At that very moment, whatever that was squeezing my head stopped. The little light of hope began to shine through the darkness that had plagued our house for so long.

As everyone was finishing up packing, I couldn't help but marvel at how everything had started to make sense. The basement steps were replaced with wood from a Native American burial ground in Missouri, the girl and her family were in Illinois, and the large memorial cross on Fort Jefferson Hill overlooked the Mississippi River and our three states. Not only this, but the same demon that was terrorizing us all, which we had seen near the cross, was traveling the river. It was interesting how it all connected.

68

The paranormal team left before the storm got real bad to where they couldn't have gotten out. Perhaps it was coincidence, but the ice storm turned out to be the worst that had ever hit our area. We went three weeks without power, heat, or anything. The national guard was even called out to distribute food and water. To conserve heat, we sealed off the living room with blankets and slept in there. We only had candles and body heat for warmth, but to our surprise, we stayed plenty warm.

I hated to see the paranormal team leave. They were on their way to the young girl that was being terribly afflicted to the point that her family called, worried for their child's safety. I hoped that they made it safely up there. Our little town seemed to have been hit the worst with the ice. Some people were bold enough to blame it on the investigators being here, and looking into the house. I personally wasn't going to believe that.

In spite of the ice storm, I was hoping that the house was clean of this demon and all other evil. Having had my hopes built up before only to have them come crashing down, I remained on the cautious side of optimistic. I also couldn't help but to remember what the medium had told us: "there would always be spirits here." All we could do was pray that it was only good ones that would come and go. If we had to have ghosts, I could live with good ones, but I didn't want anymore to do with the bad.

Mulling it over in my mind, I thought of all the different water ways in town, and how each ran to the river. The thought of us never being rid of the spirits made me want to just walk out of the home that we were so proud of. How could we live and be happy in our home, not knowing if we could live in peace? Would we have to worry about being listened to over the phone where we would so often hear growling? Also, it bothered me that we weren't able to find out who "Prisoner 910" was. I was hopeful that it was a passing spirit and not the demon playing tricks.

69

Thankfully, we made it through the ice storm without freezing or going hungry. We didn't have any lights, water, or gas for about three weeks. At night, John would crank up the generator so we could watch a few movies and escape from reality a while. The kids would occupy themselves with their gaming consoles. There wasn't a whole lot of getting out during that time. Living on a hill, it was difficult to get down the driveway without sliding off into the creek beyond. I worried about my mother most of all during this time. I was slightly relieved that her sister had got to mom's house before this had all hit. At the very least, I was glad she wasn't alone.

The medium that was with the paranormal team told me that if there was anything he could do, to give him a call. I saved his number, but thankfully, the house was quiet at that time. To help ensure that the blessing took, Father Luke had left a prayer for me to say everyday after they left. I kept it on the refrigerator and prayed it each day. I had no intentions of taking any chances.

70

It had been a few months since the ice storm. Thank God, people around our area had pulled together to help the elderly and the poor, who had no other way to help themselves. I wanted so badly for us to get our lives back to the way it was before we moved to the house on Beech Grove. I kept myself busy, trying to help my mother. She called every day after the first time she heard the growling over the phone. She would often warn us to get out of the house and that if it were up to her, she would burn the place down.

I would repeatedly tell her to not say such things, out of fear that it might happen at night, and we wouldn't be able to escape in time. However, at the age of eighty-one, it was difficult to keep my mom quiet. She would tell me that she wasn't afraid, which was well and good, but she wasn't the one that lived there.

71

One day, my son called. While he was with his dad, John had a heart attack, and was being air lifted to the hospital. My thoughts raced back to the medium, when he had first entered our house. I remembered how he had gripped his chest and told my husband to take care of himself. He asked if John had trouble with his heart in the past, which at that time, he had not. The signs were so clear, and yet, this whole event had blindsided me.

I rushed to the hospital, hoping that my husband would be okay. There I thankfully found that he would be fine. I was told that the emergency crew had given him around twenty shots of morphine while in the helicopter. They had tried everything that they could to ease his pain, but to no avail. Finally, they told him they could give him one more experimental drug that might help, but he had to ask the doctor first.

Thankfully, the heart doctor told them they might as well, because if they didn't, he would certainly die. Thank God, the drug worked. Just recovering from a terrible virus that had nearly left me too weak to walk, I prayed I would make it down to see my husband. I feared that he wasn't going to make it through this, with how serious that they made it sound, and I had to be with him.

Two weeks prior to his heart attack, he had been working and took a nasty hit to his leg. It looked and hurt so bad, that he even went to the doctor to have it checked, without me having to nag him. My mother had wanted to see it too, because her second husband had gotten hit in his leg before having a heart attack. Her concern, which turned out to be justified, was that John would have the same thing happen to him.

We told her that he had already been to the doctor and he had told John to stay off that leg for a while. Of course, being told to do something and actually listening to the advice were two different things. I could no more get him to listen than I could get a cow to operate a VCR. After he escaped his brush with death, he went on to spend two weeks in the hospital. Later on, he would tell me that the pain he felt in the helicopter was so bad, that he had begged God to take him rather than endure another minute.

72

While coming home one day, after visiting John at the hospital, I noticed a lot of smoke coming from town, around where my mother lived. As I got closer, all I could see were fire trucks. It turned out that my mother's house had caught fire. Immediately, I was concerned that she hadn't escaped in time, but thankfully, a neighbor had noticed the smoke while out for a walk, and rushed into her house to save her. I still cannot fully express my gratitude for what he did.

By the time I arrived on the scene, half of the house had already collapsed in. As we sat across the street, watching memories and everything she owned go up in smoke, I thought of all the times she had told me over the phone to burn down our place and walk away. With her house in flames, I wondered if whatever was in the house had heard her and took revenge. It sounds crazy I suppose, but we'll never know.

At the age of eighty-one, mama never recovered from losing everything she had. Hoping to ease her pain, I told her that the things we have in this world aren't ours but for a short time anyway. Loosing things like photos and items that held the precious memories of her children when they were young, and the children she had lost, was what hurt the most. Each day after the fire, mama seemed to slip further away.

The best we could, we replaced everything that was lost. My brother and sister even went and bought her a brand new bedroom set. She remarked it was nice, but ended up never using it once. Instead, she would sleep on the couch; mama just never was the same.

73

About a month away from Thanksgiving, I told mama that I would come and cook Thanksgiving dinner at her new place. The idea seemed to perk her up a bit. One day a little later on, I was fixing her a lunch when she asked, "Nancy, do you think that the thing that was in your house heard us talking over the phone and that's what made my house burn down?"

I had never voiced my suspicions to her about that. I did my best to reassure her and ease her mind on the subject. While I spoke, I could see in my mind the foot tall flame that had tried to creep its way down our telephone wire to our house. Mama would lay on the couch almost all the time, would hardly eat, and didn't need any more on her mind than she already had. We did everything in the world for her, but none of it was enough.

74

On November the fifth, with her surviving children gathered around her, my mother passed away. In the moments prior, my brother Pat called us to say that he thought mama had a stroke. We rushed to get to her place, arriving before the ambulance. Walking in, we found her sitting upright on the couch, staring straight ahead. As I bent down in front of her, I could see a single tear run down her face. Gently wiping it away, it took everything in my power to not fall to pieces. It was like she had waited for Ruth and I to arrive before she could leave. She took two deep breaths, let out a holler, and died.

My grandson Joseph was an EMT then. When he walked through the door, he hugged me, then turned to my mother. He knew she was gone, but still tried to bring her back. As they took mama away, it was hard to believe that she was gone. We all knew that she had been slowly dying, but we were hoping for just one last Thanksgiving and Christmas. I think that after her house burnt, she made her peace with God and was ready to go home.

She had told us kids more than once that if anything happened to her, we weren't to be upset. She wanted us to be thankful that she was on the other side with her children. I tried my best to honor her wishes, but it was so hard to do.

More than anything, I began to worry about my brother Charles, who had lived with mama his entire life. When the rest of us weren't around, it fell to him to take care of her the best he could. Never once did he complain. At her funeral, he never went too close to the casket. I watched him keep his distance, looking at mama laying in her casket with tears in his eyes.

Not wanting him to be alone, I asked Charles to come and stay with us. My efforts were dampened though by past events. To begin with, mama had told him about our house being haunted. He didn't fully believe her at first. One day he had come to spend the day with me. Having health issues, he would occasionally have to lay down. That day in particular, I invited him to go and lay down in our room. After only a few minutes, Charles came out of the bedroom and went zipping past me. Without so much as a "goodbye," he went straight out the door and went home.

Later I found out he had told mama that while he was laying on the bed, the computer keyboard flew around the room and landed right back where it was. I considered he might have been imagining the whole ordeal. All the same, there was something about that computer. Perhaps it was because it was in the basement. I do know that about a week after we had brought the computer upstairs, I had one of the creepiest experiences ever with that piece of junk.

I was busy making my bed, when the computer came on all by itself. What made that so bad, was what it came up with. On the screen was some kind of witchcraft or devil page: a black screen with what looked like blood running down it. Written on the page were the words, "Death Clock." Not interested in finding out what that meant, I quickly unplugged the computer and threw it in the trash. I didn't want to risk giving it to anyone, and I haven't had another computer since.

I talked to Charles and told him the house was okay now, and the computer was gone. He asked what happened to it, and I told him that it quite working so I threw it out. Finally, about a week after mama passed, Charles came over for a visit. He started by only staying for a few minutes at a time, but after a while, he got to where he wasn't bothered to stay the night.

75

It was typical for Charles to get up early in the morning. The second night that he stayed, he was sitting, enjoying a cup of coffee at the dinner table. I was working on something in the living room when I heard the sound of running water. Thinking that my brother had went into the bathroom and left the water running, I called out to him. I was confused, having expected his voice to come from the bathroom, when he answered me from the kitchen.

I got up and walked out of the living room to find Charles sitting at the table with a funny look on his face. Turning to the other side, I saw the kitchen sink was on full blast. I asked if he had turned it on, but he said he hadn't. I went over and turned the water off. When I turned back around, Charles was putting his coat on. He told me he would see me later, and left. It seemed like any time someone new stayed in the house, whatever spirits that were there would act up and scare our guest away.

76

It looked like we might be the next couple to up and leave the house on Beech Grove Road. I truly was beginning to believe that if we didn't leave, one of us would be the next family member to be buried. Due to health problems, John hadn't been able to work in years. After a while, I couldn't work either, and at times, could barely walk. On top of everything else, the house had begun to have a dark feeling building up once again.

It was almost like whatever was in the house was playing a game with us. I was certain that the dark spirits were. At times, it felt like they were even trying to get inside of us. A terrible, oppressive, pressure would occasionally over come me, and I would get these invasive thoughts to take drastic action of one type or another. I didn't like talking about it. Even though I knew I was stronger than them, I didn't want to tempt them to push any further.

More than anything, I wanted them out of our home. We had seemingly tried everything, with nothing providing a lasting solution. I continued on in my stance that someone had left a door open, and that door had to be closed. I would just have to keep trying to find a way, until one or the other of us lost.

77

Charles, to my surprise, came back to spend the night with us. He had been so lonely since mama died. On the upside, he was talking to us more than he ever had before, which I saw as promising. In the morning, we sat and drank coffee together before he left to go home. He would always get up and say, "I guess I better get on Nancy. I'll see you later." I knew he would be back in a few hours. I wanted to ask if he wanted to stay with us every night; I felt so sorry for Charles.

Right after he left, my husband got up and asked if Charles was okay this morning. Asking him why, he told me that it sounded like Charles was walking around the house last night, fell, then went back to bed. Apparently, John went to check on him, and finding him in bed, was told he was fine. Thinking it was curious, but no big deal, I let it go, and never brought it up to Charles.

78

I had been waking up early in the morning for some time. Some mornings, I would be up as early as two-thirty or three o'clock. After a while, I started hearing a man's voice. It seemed to be only a few words, but I would always hear my name. It began when John and my nephew Al started cleaning out the basement.

One particular morning, I was woke up by knocking. Right after the knocking, I hear the sound of someone walking in the dark hallway. I decided to quietly get up and flip the hallway light switch that was just outside our bedroom door. I flipped the switch: nothing happened. For some reason, I felt more uneasy than usual. Over time, I had gotten used to things happening in the house, but this seemed different.

At the other end of the hall, the kitchen light was shinning just enough to dimly illuminate the hall. Slowly, I peaked around the corner of our door towards the kitchen. I shuddered in fear as I choked back a scream. Standing at the end of the hall was a shadow figure that was clearer and more defined than anything I had ever seen before. It was as if it was there just so I would see it. In its left hand, swinging freely by its side, the figure seemed to be holding something.

Without any warning, I saw the figure throw whatever was in his hand right at me. Instinctively, I ducked, but the hit never came. As I looked back towards him, the shadow darted down the hall towards me, disappearing as soon as it drew near. No sooner had it vanished, the bathroom door slammed shut. I stood still, held in place by the silence that filled the hall.

We had been through so much at that house, I thought nothing could scare me anymore: until that very moment. I thought that maybe this was the shadow that I had seen in the bathroom right after we moved in, or perhaps this was "Prisoner 910." Maybe it was just a spirit that was passing though, just as the medium said would happen. One thing was for certain: nothing was ever going to change in that house. We would either have to put up with it all or leave.

79

No matter what we did to the house, it always felt the same way: dark and dead. The house, or rather what's there, continued to drain us. I can safely say that we were no longer the people who had moved there. If only people knew what we had been through, they might pay more attention in their own lives.

We used to be strong, but over time have been worn down. Maybe that's why the spirits of the house had kept us there. People continue to ask why we didn't move, but the facts remain the same: we couldn't. Now all we own is the house and what dwells within. Truth be told, I think that we are the ones visiting: the house is really theirs.

80

I don't think I can include everything that has happened in this house. Many of the things, no one would believe. We had been scratched, assaulted, thrown out of bed, had our hair pulled, and so much more. We have heard a whole slew of voices and growls. I have woken up to dark shadows standing at the foot of the bed, some have stood over me, and a few have seemingly tried to suck the breath right out of me. Then, just as you think that's everything, something will be hurled at you.

Having lived in this house, I am a firm believer that there are spirits, both good and bad, around us everyday. They are here, walking this earth, just behind the veil of this world. I have seen them both inside and outside of my home. Just like many people, I didn't always believe, but I do now.

When you think you have seen something out of the corner of your eye, next time, you might want to check again; you might not be as alone as you think. Make no mistake, there are things that are in the dark and things that go bump in the night, and your belief is not required. Choosing not to believe will not save you. Even if you don't believe in them, they believe in you.

Timeline of Pertinent Events

- 1780- Fort Jefferson is built.
- 1781- Chickasaw attack and massacre at Fort Jefferson.
- 1803 November 14-20- Lewis and Clark camp near and visit site of Fort Jefferson.
- 1964- House is built.
- 1964- Dillon Dubois (~6) drowns in pond near house. Parents were one of the first owners of the house.
- 1970's- (exact date unknown) John's niece (7) dies.
- 1973 September 17- Nancy's brother Matthew (20) dies in car wreck.
- 1980's- Piano couple lived in house.
- 1992- Joseph (2) is saved from the broken window by unseen force.
- 1997- Nancy and John purchase the house.
  - » Burns witchcraft book that was found in basement.
  - » One month after moving in, both Nancy and John report being chronically tired and gas company checks for leaks (none found).
  - » Around same time, Nancy has sighting in bathroom.
  - » Roughly two months after moving in: Sarah was attacked in basement.

- 1998 to 1999- Nancy starts keeping diaries after Daisy's first experience.

- 1999 June 14- Nancy's brother Frank's birthday party and Daisy's (52) suicide.

- 1999 June 17- Daisy's body recovered from Mississippi River.

- 1999 July 8- Nancy has first encounter with demon. Lasts an hour and it lets her go at 0300

- 2003- Rachel (5) sees little girl that resembles John's deceased niece in backyard, sees the figure with colorful horns, and the wire fire incident.

  » Nick (6) experiences sleep paralysis type symptoms in living room.

  » Steven (8) claims to have an "imaginary" friend in the house that's afraid of the light.

- 2007- Sherry and Carly have incident with basement door.

- 2007 June 20- Nancy's brother Greg (66) dies by suicide.

- 2008 November- Nancy and Joseph see demon after driving past Fort Jefferson Cross.

- 2009- Carly sees hag-like woman in hall outside bathroom.

- 2009 January- One member from the team arrives to evaluate situation.

- 2009 January 22- Paranormal team arrives.

- 2009 January 26- Ice storm arrives.

- 2009 March 23- TV episode aired.

- 2010 April 28- Nancy's friend dies from cancer.

- 2010 April 29- Nancy sees a black mist in her room and learns that a friend just died of cancer.

- 2011 February 28- Nancy and her pet Yorkie feel presence in the bedroom and feels her head being "squeezed."

- 2011 November 5- Nancy's mom (81) dies.

- 2013 December 22- Nancy's brother Charles (54) dies in flash flood.

- 2014- After years of developing health problems, Nancy finds out she has cancer.

- 2015 August- Neighbor who saved Nancy's mother from house fire is shot and killed.

- 2016 April 19- Jackie (37) dies under suspicious circumstances.

- 2018 April 20- Daisy's son George (48) is found dead under suspicious circumstances.

- 2019 March 13- Nancy's brother Pat (68) dies.

- 2021 April 18- Nancy (66 years old and having been married 52 years) dies.

Before the Haunting

As one may have gathered by the accounts of the preceding pages, the haunting of the house on Beech Grove wasn't the first time in Nancy's life that she had encountered strange, even paranormal, events. Starting with her childhood, she lived through some bone-chilling events. As the events predominantly afflicted her sister Ruth, Nancy remained a skeptic towards the supernatural.

Not talked about as much in this text, or the source material, are the events that took place in the trailer they were living in, prior to the house. These incidents were a further build up to the crescendo of terror that awaited them. The trailer itself was placed on the site their previous house sat on, only a short distance away from the house that is the focus above. Just as Nancy's mother would face years later, their first house was also reduced to a cinder.

To more completely convey what these days were like, we have decided to include the few entries Nancy had made on these incidents. It may be worth noting by the reader, that in the trailer, just as with her childhood home, the majority of these occurrences happen to others. Furthermore, aside from the near-death of her grandson, the majority of these events are quite tame compared to what she would experience later on.

1

It was mid-summer when my niece, Sharon came to stay with us. At seven, she was full of energy and just loved to play. The first day she was there, we played with every toy in the house before we went outside to play in the little pool we had set up. It wasn't anything glamorous, but it allowed her to splash and cool off from the baking heat.

By the end of the day, I was wore out and glad to see bedtime come: both hers and mine. I was sound asleep until about midnight, when I was awakened by a soft voice calling my name. With great effort, I opened my tired eyes to see Sharon standing beside my bed. I asked her what was wrong. "There's a man in the backyard." She said quietly.

I was now wide awake. "What?"

"I got up to get a drink of water, and there was a funny-looking man in the backyard."

Asking her what she meant by "funny-looking," she told me that he looked like a normal person, but like he was see through. At this, I was a little bit relieved and started to think she had just dreamed it all. I got up out of bed and went with her to the back patio door so she could show me where the man was. Seeing nothing, I told her it was nothing and, having gotten her a drink, took her back to bed.

Early the next morning, Sharon got up as I was making breakfast. Rubbing her eyes, she came in and sat at the table. Asking her if she had slept well, I couldn't help but joke about the incident the night before. Despite my humor, she remained adamant about what she had seen. Finally, I said, "Well tell me what he looked like." She told me it looked like she could see right through him, but she could tell that he was wearing camouflage. She also said he was just standing there, like he was lost, and then he just disappeared. More amused than anything, I told her not to think any more about it, and I was sure she wouldn't be seeing him again.

2

Another busy day was winding down by the time my husband walked in the door one evening. While telling me about his day, John started back towards our bedroom at the end of the hall. Mid-sentence, he stopped talking. After a brief pause, I heard him calling my name, telling me to "come here."

I got off the couch and noticed that John had frozen in his tracks in front of the middle bedroom. In this bedroom we kept all the kids toys and used it as a kind of playroom. Reaching his side, I asked what the matter was. He asked if any of the kids were there. Confused, I told him the only ones there, was us.

Asking what was wrong, I could see his hair starting to raise on end. "I could swear that I just saw one of the kids in here as I was walking past. I backed up right quick to take another look, and there was no one there, but a ball that was still rolling. Are you sure none of the kids are here?"

I told him I was sure the kids weren't there (and I was a little worried he wasn't either). I told him he was just tired and needed to get some rest. As he continued to the bedroom, I gave a quick look into the play room before turning off the light and going back to the couch. I tried to believe the explanation I gave John, but couldn't help being a bit freaked out about the whole experience.

3

I'm beginning to wonder if there wasn't something to what Sharon had seen. Early one morning, right after I had woke up, I heard someone knocking on the sliding glass door. Curious as to who could be knocking on our door so early, I went to see who it was. Nearing the door, I briefly caught a glimpse of a man in a camouflage jacket as he appeared to fade from the dim light of the window.

Hesitating a moment, I went to the door to ask who was there. Turning on the porch light, I could see no one. I kept staring towards the light's edge, trying eagerly to get a glimpse at what may be beyond. Questioning what I had seen, I couldn't think of a logical explanation for what had happened. Suddenly, I found myself remembering Sharon's experience when she was staying with us. Had we seen the same thing?

4

My daughter Sherry and her husband Russ are staying with us for a while. It should only be temporary until they can find a place to call their own. It's been kind of nice to have them here, even though the trailer is a bit cramped. One day, it wasn't the close quarters that got to me. At breakfast, Sherry came up to me and asked what had been going on the night before. Asking what she meant, what she told me left me at a loss.

"About eleven last night, Russ and I were asleep in our room. I woke up first, thinking that you guys were fighting. It sounded like you two were about to knock each other out or worse. Russ woke up and asked if everything was alright. Not knowing what to expect, I got up and headed to your room. When I got there, I didn't hear anything: no yelling, no fighting, nothing. Worried, I cracked the door open to find both of you fast asleep. What was that all about?"

I had no clue. I wanted to tell her anything, but couldn't find the words. There wasn't anything I could say, really. We hadn't been fighting, nor did we hear anything. I couldn't explain it away, other than to ask if maybe she had dreamed it all. Russ then brought up the point that she couldn't have dreamed it, because he heard it too. I didn't want to say anything to them, but I was starting to notice that, every-so-often, something strange would happen here. Not wanting to seem crazy, I kept my suspicions to myself.

5

My little two year old grandson Joseph came to stay with us for a few days. It was great to have him racing around the house. It reminded me of the days when John and I had little ones of our own. Family is one of the greatest blessings in life. Even so, they can also scare you to death.

While Joseph was playing in the house, John and I were talking in the kitchen. I had seen Joseph was playing by the window with some toys. Between glances, John and I heard the sound of glass breaking. Immediately, we looked over to Joseph. As soon as I saw him, my heart dropped. Somehow, Joseph had broke the window and his head was now precariously placed through the hole. The jagged glass circled his neck like the teeth of a hungry predator ready to sink into its prey. All it would have took was one false move, and I knew he would be dead. My heart in my throat, I told him not to move. With how his head was positioned, I was worried how we were going to free him. As we swiftly moved towards him, we watched in amazement as his head was gently maneuvered back through, as if guided by an invisible hand. Each movement was too smooth and precise to have simply been him.

I didn't care what it was, I was simply thankful he was unharmed. I dropped to my knees and held him in my arms as I checked him for any injuries. Amazingly, he barely had a scratch. We came close to losing Joseph that day, but I feel confident that something saved him. I am certain that had anyone else seen what happened, they would feel the same way.

6

We were almost completely done with the trailer and in the new house. All we lacked were moving a couple of boxes and to get the trailer sold. Having forgot to pick up the boxes on his way home from work, we decided to go by after dinner. As we pulled up that evening, we noticed that the light was on in the kitchen. Not thinking anything of it, we went in, grabbed the boxes, turned off the light, and got loaded into the truck.

Just as John was getting into the truck, he stopped. "Didn't we turn that light off before coming out?"

"What light?" I asked. John pointed towards the trailer, and sure enough, the kitchen light was back on. Sliding out of the truck, John went back in to turn off the light. From the truck I could see the light turn off. A few seconds later, he was back at the truck and we were ready to go. As we started to back out, I noticed the light coming from the trailer. The truck jolted to a stop as I told my husband. "I guess something doesn't want us to leave." I joked.

This time, I decided to go with him. Standing at the door of the trailer, I watched as he walked in and hit the switch one more time. As he started out the door, he turned back and said into the darkness, "Now I'm not doing this all night! Keep the light off! If you want to come along, then let's go, but don't touch that light." A cold chill ran up our spines. Something told me that was not a good thing to say. Too late now I suppose.

Corroborating Tales of Terror

In the process of uncovering further facets of the haunting on Beech Grove, we were able to gather two types of stories from the first-hand witnesses. The first of these were independent accounts of events that were recorded by Nancy in her diaries. The second type of story was not recorded by Nancy, but added further depth to the mystery of the property. In this section in particular, we will only be including events that occurred within the time frame covered by Nancy's diaries.

In one incident[1], Sherry and Carly were walking into the home after going shopping one afternoon. On entering the home, they began to hear heavy footsteps coming from the basement. Naturally, they began to wonder if someone had broken in, or even if what they were hearing was real. Before they could try to reason or run, a ferocious banging was heard against the basement door.

Without a moments hesitation, Sherry threw herself against the door. With all her might, she stood strong against whatever was trying to break through. Mere feet away, Carly could see clearly the hollow door bow out with each hit. Preparing for anything, they steeled themselves for what may come next. Then, as quickly as it started: silence.

Scared witless, the two trembled in anticipation for the next attack. After a couple of agonizing minutes passed without a sound, Sherry gestured to the back door. At her signal, they ran out of the house and called John to tell him what had just happened. Sitting

---

1. Subject 2, Interviewed by Blankenship and Johnson, 16 Oct. 2024

in their car, they waited to see if anyone would run out from the house, but nothing happened. They knew that no one could have come in through the basement, as it had been sealed shut, so anyone running out would have to come out via the top floor.

When John arrived, he went in to look throughout house. Searching high and low, there wasn't even a trace of anyone else having been in the house. When Sherry and Carly went in, they opened the door to the basement, expecting to find some sign of the beating it took. Like two detectives, they looked over the door. To their surprise, they didn't find a mark of any kind.

On another occasion[2], not long before the paranormal teams arrival, Carly was in the home alone. She had been staying there off and on as a guest of the family. While in the bathroom, she started to hear the sound of heavy steps in the hallway. They sounded as if someone was walking barefoot out of the kitchen, towards the bedrooms.

She first thought how strange it was that she hadn't heard anyone else come home. Turning to see who it was, she found herself petrified by what was passing before her. Moving slowly past the bathroom door was the hunched figure of a tall, frail woman. She appeared to have elongated arms and legs, attached delicately to a pale frame that was smeared with darkness. Her long dark hair, thin and wet, clung like algae to her shoulders.

Terrified, Carly watched as she passed down the hall, one thudding step at a time. Excruciating seconds passed before Carly could move. Working up her courage, she inched to the door. To her relief, and as with so many other instances, she found no one and nothing there. Another image gone by, only to live in the mind of its beholder.

---

2. Subject 1, Interviewed by Blankenship and Johnson, 16 Oct. 2024

The Haunting Continues

As indicated in the main text, Nancy's story didn't exactly play out like the movies. If it were all some fanciful story, the house blessing would have worked and everyone would live happily-ever-after. Unfortunately, real-life has its own rules. While the most severe events ceased, we were able to find out for ourselves that the medium was indeed correct: "there will always be spirits in the house."

Taking up the position of skeptics with inquiring minds, we set about taking various steps in order to give this story the fair, objective exam it deserved. With what access we could gain, we worked to investigate for ourselves, the people and places that were involved. Out of respect to them, their names have been changed herein to protect their privacy.

Among the eyewitness accounts uncovered in our search, were details of select events that happened after the final entries Nancy made. To begin with, was the inevitable fallout that followed the airing of the episode which featured the house and the family. In the immediate wake of the show, John and Nancy saw a noticeable decrease in the number of people who would stop in to visit. Following this, was the inevitable gawking of people who would trickle by to get a look at the haunted house from TV. Even to this day, there are people who will go slowly past, or even stop and take photos of the house.

Behind the facade of the unassuming house, out of the view of prying eyes, the haunting continued. Some of the worst of the activity was kept at bay by Nancy's faithful daily recitation of *The*

Warrior's Prayer. This prayer was given to her by Father Luke after the completion of the blessing of their home. Keeping the prayer under a magnet on the fridge door, Nancy was sure to repeat it everyday. Even so, events continued to unfold.

Several years had passed since the house was investigated. One day, Carly, her little girl Madison, and Rachel were all sitting together on the front porch. While Madison sat in her little rocking chair and played, the conversation between Carly and Rachel turned to the crazy things that had happened in the house. Thinking it might be fun, the ill-advised suggestion was made to use a make-shift Ouija board, and see if anything would answer them.

The two took turns asking questions, but nothing happened. They lightheartedly laughed it off. It seemed the spirits weren't in the mood to talk, they joked. As they continued to talk and watch Madison play, they watched as Madison, without the least warning, was forcefully pushed over backwards in her chair. Rushing over, Carly picked up her daughter and made sure she wasn't hurt. Looking up as she embraced her child, she caught the worried eyes of Rachel. Clearly, whatever the spirits didn't want to say with words, they said with action.

Years after this, perhaps one of the most surprising and welcome witnesses had an experience: a die-hard skeptic. While this sighting occurred in the presence of others, his view is the most compelling. Bert, a friend of the family, is an atheist and skeptic in the paranormal. To mention anything on such topics would be met with a look of derision, at best.

One morning, around 0830, while talking with John at the table, Bert asked who the man was in the gray coat. Confused, John asked, what man he was talking about. Bert then proceeded to say that he had seen a man in a gray coat, with a mustache, and long ear lobes. Thinking that his friend was pulling his leg, John laughed and told him there wasn't anyone who looked like that there. Even so, Bert insisted that he had seen the man, not once, but multiple times in the house.

While his sightings haven't contributed to any major shift in his beliefs (yet), it is among the most important accounts for at least three reasons. First, he is an ardent skeptic, to say the least. Secondly, what he sees has been seen by other independent witnesses. Third, at least a couple of these witnesses, Bert included, have seen this apparition on multiple occasions.

Evidence of Our Own

Being keen to inquire, and interview all the usual suspects (living and deceased), we took it upon ourselves to go looking for evidence of our own. As stated previously, it was with skeptical minds that we had to approach these events. After all, it is much more difficult to put effort into anything that may prove a waste of one's resources. Not to spoil the ending, but the efforts have been well worth while.

In between the examination of supporting historical events and a mound of correlating data, we grabbed up what gear we had to investigate, and took a journey into the unknown. Having done some "ghost hunting" prior to this investigation, we were first and foremost careful to scrutinize ourselves and our methodologies to get the most unbiased results possible. It is our aspiration to be able to present the evidence in full via an appropriate medium in the future. Dealing within the limitations of print, we will do what we can.

To begin with, our main means of investigation were digital cameras, recorders, and thermal cameras. Not wanting to give room for the immediate dismissal of evidence, we tried to stay away from the use of phones as they could become the source of interference. Next, we were careful to be mindful of anything that could create a false result or contamination of the recordings. To remedy this, we came up with the simple, yet effective system of placing the recorder in one place, maintaining distance, and verbally noting any explainable sound happening in the moment.

Regarding our results with the camera, we were careful to debunk what anomalies we could. As with the recordings, we expect the reader to maintain their skepticism. Never-the-less, we hope all minds remain open to the possibility of what we present here being evidence of something beyond our common understanding. Included in the photo section of this book, besides shots from our investigations, are photos from the sites mentioned in this text.

Note: These are only selections of the evidence gathered. Though more evidence exists, we have only included these to demonstrate we were, in fact, able to find evidence which points to the presence of the supernatural, thus lending credence to the overall story.

SELECT AUDIO CAPTURES

As it's hard to hear audio on paper, we have elected to recount our findings by presenting select descriptions of captures from our recordings. It isn't hard to argue that this is by far one of the least perfect ways to present such evidence, but this will have to do until the evidence will be given the chance to speak for itself.

In the first recording, we are standing in the cemetery where Nancy and Jackie are buried. While asking questions and giving an opportunity for something to answer, a blood-curdling scream can be heard in the distance. Granted, this sound, while frightening to hear, was not heard by us or by the dogs at a neighboring house.

The dogs here, are the best backers of this evidence for at least two reasons. The first reason is that, while we could be choosing to ignore the sound to let it pass as evidence, dogs have no ulterior motives. Second, we know that the dogs would have reacted to the sound, if it was from natural origin, because they could be heard barking at various other points in the recording. One final, yet separate point to keep from debunking this evidence, is the absence of large cats or other creatures in our area that could make such a howl.

The second recording is better still. To be more precise, we were able to capture what was perhaps the best example of a

"Grade A" EVP (electronic voice phenomenon), that we have had the privilege to capture. To add to its brilliance as a piece of evidence, it happened in a spot we had just captured a light anomaly (picture included herein). The site was the memorial wall in front of the Fort Jefferson Hill Cross.

First off, the light anomaly was at first thought to be a lens flare, but was unable to be recreated in subsequent photos. Intrigued by this, we placed the recorder by the wall, near the portion we captured the light anomaly. In the recording, we are heard asking, "Was that you we got a picture of?" Aside from this, only some other slight superfluous sounds could be heard. During the long pause after we asked this, a clear, "yes" could be heard. Such a small word, but enough to make standing in the cold air that night worth it.

PHOTOGRAPHIC CAPTURES

Evidence much easier to convey by book, is photographic evidence. Even though we could write a jumble of words for these photos, we will let the photos speak for themselves. After all, "a picture is worth a thousand words," and it's time to give weary fingers a rest. To ensure a better impact of each photo, however, we will include a few brief words to give context.

Note: To keep the book organized, this section will include all of the photos most pertinent to this work. For more, please visit our team page on Facebook, TikTok, and more, under the name: Veil Breakers Paranormal Research and Investigations.

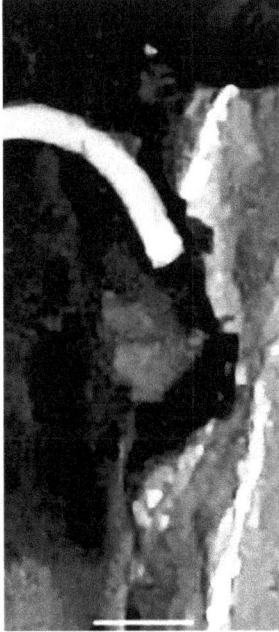

Original photo of a face captured in the woods behind the house.

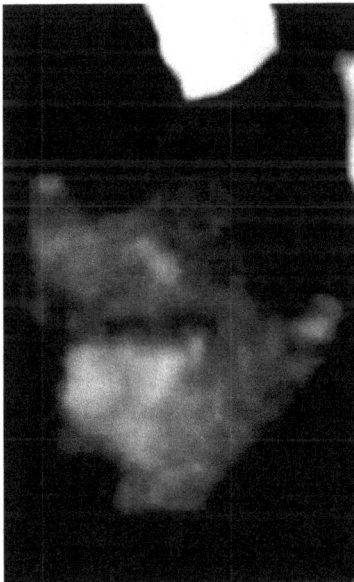

Close-up of face in figure 1.

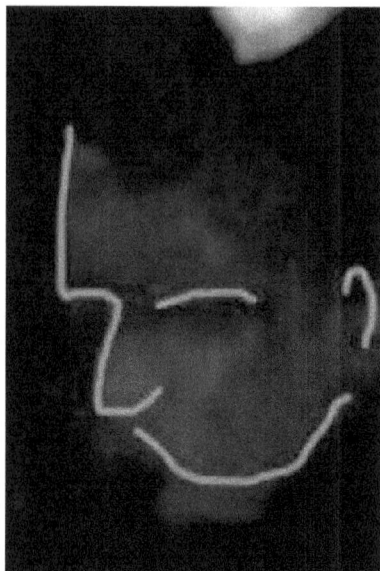

Face in previous photos with emphasized features.

Wide shot of light anomaly captured near the memorial wall
on Fort Jefferson Hill.

Close-up of light anomaly in last image.

Wide shot depicting terrain between the cross and river below.

Close-up of cliff to emphasize height. Daisy's autopsy showed no broken
bones or significant injuries.

The Warrior's Prayer

Heavenly Father your warrior prepares for battle Today I claim Victory over Satan by putting on the whole Armor of God.

I put on the *Girdle of Truth!* May I stand firm in the truth of your Word so I will not be a victim of Satan's lies,

I put on the *Breastplate of Righteousness!* May it guard my heart from evil so it will remain pure and holy protected under the blood of Jesus Christ.

I put on the *Shoes of Peace!* May I stand firm in the Good News of the Gospel so your peace will shine through me and be a light to all I encounter.

I take the *Shield of Faith!* May I be ready for Satan's fiery doubt, denieal and deceit so I will not be vulnerable to spiritual defeat.

I put on the *Helmet of Salvation.* May I keep my mind focused on you so Satan will not have a stronghold on my thoughts.

I take the *Sword of the Spirit.* May the two edged sword of your Word be ready in my hands so I can expose the tempting words of Satan.

By faith your warrior has put on the whole Amour of God! I am prepared to live this day in spiritual Victory. Amen

The exact prayer Father Luke gave to Nancy.

Topographical map of Wickliffe, Kentucky, with emphasis on burial mounds and cross location.

The History

Much as Nancy ran into, the efforts to find out more about the property were hard going. The rumors and other subjective accounts that she gathered, and we uncovered during our investigation, were good to start with, but were not as solid as a paper trail. Even when accounts of various events were found to reliably match between independent witnesses, we still were left searching for more.

From this desire, we turned our attention to the history of the surrounding area. There, our quest was to explore the underlying stories that, over time, would provide the threads that stitched together the parts of a greater tale. From the hints taken from Nancy's diary entries, we delved into what history we could find, focusing on two points in particular, that might help explain the events that plagued her and those she loved.

While we also did more extensive research into the areas of the science of the paranormal, the psychology of unexplained phenomena, and the like, we chose to place those in a second book that will follow this one. We thought of them as being too significant to squeeze into the second half of this book. Furthermore, in honor of Nancy, we did not want to detract from the story she worked so hard to compile.

THE FORT: MASSACRES AND MEMORIALS

First, we turned our attention to the history of one of the central locations that is featured in this story: Fort Jefferson. Conceived by the mind of Governor Patrick Henry of Virginia, Fort Jefferson was built in 1780 by George Rogers Clark.[1] The fort was established at the confluence of the Ohio and Mississippi for two main reasons. First, the position of the fort, along with other forts that would occupy the area, such as Holt and Defiance, was key for the defense of the territory against British led attacks by tribes of Native Americans. Second, the early fort gave further weight of the projected claim to the colonies' holding of territory at the western boundary of the Mississippi River.[2]

In the year of 1781, the Chickasaws, led by a Scotchman named Colbert, laid siege to the fort for five days. The tribe was incensed by the occupants of the fort, who were unable to get supplies, hunting on and otherwise using tribal land, against formerly agreed upon terms. Many of the settlers were killed by either the Chickasaws or from the lack of supplies. Finally, General Clark arrived with reinforcements and supplies. Not long after the massacre, the fort was left abandoned for many years.[3]

From the fourteenth to the twentieth of November in 1803, Clark's younger brother, William Clark (of Lewis and Clark), would make camp not far from the site.[4] Among their other tasks such as charting positions, scouting for possible sites for new forts, and so forth, they would also visit the former fort. By this time there was a fairly steady peace between the whites and the local tribes, but there was no clearing away the blood that had long since stained the soil. It would be nearly two hundred years before the

1. Society, Kentucky Historical. "Fort Jefferson Site." Kentucky Historical Society, Kentucky Historical Society, 2024, history.ky.gov/markers/fort-jefferson-site.

2. Contributors, Multiple. Lewis & Clark Corps of Discovery, 1803-1806: The Greatest Exploration in the Nation's History. Back Home In Kentucky, Inc., 2003.

3. Society, Ibid

4. Contributors, Ibid

ninety foot tall cross would be erected on Fort Jefferson Hill. It was shortly after its completion that Daisy would park her car there, and sadly decide to walk into the river.

Here, the keen reader might have connected the intriguing fact that the massacre started because the Chickasaws were unhappy with the unauthorized use of their land, with at least one correlating factor: the basement stairs. Even though the lumber was taken from woods next to a tribal burial ground that was in Missouri, it doesn't matter as the territory of the mound builders blanketed the area and then some from circa 1000-1750 AD.[5] This one factor alone, we agree, is interesting, but doesn't make a case. For this reason, we move towards the next section of "coincidences."

NATIVE LORE AND MORE

Each tribe of Native-Americans have a set of beliefs that are unique to themselves, while often having similarities shared with other tribes. The Chickasaws and Choctaws, for instance, both have tales of a "great horned serpent" called "Sint-Holo." While not strictly "evil" as we would classify it, they did believe this spirit was dangerous and could "drag people to a watery death."[6] What's more, is that these spirits are known by one name or another among tribes in the eastern US and into Canada; traveling only occasionally on land, but mainly in freshwater lakes and rivers.[7]

Unlike many other spirit-creatures of tribal lore, these horned serpents do not seem to mirror a naturally found animal. Instead, they are depicted in natural ways, but are highly supernatural in character, having abilities such as shape-shifting, invisibility, or

5. Survey, Kentucky Archaeological. "Wickliffe Mounds State Historic Site." Discover Kentucky Archaeology., Commonwealth of Kentucky, 2022, archaeology.ky.gov/Find-a-Site/Pages/ Wickliffe.aspx.

6. "Native American Legends: Sint-Holo." Native Languages of the Americas, 1998, www.native-languages.org/morelegends/sint-holo.htm.

7. "Native American Horned Serpents of Myth and Legend." Native Languages of the Americas, 1998–2020, https://www. native-languages.org/horned -serpent.htm

hypnosis.[8] Additionally, these serpent-like spirits, are said to have the power to control storms and weather.[9] While we are tempted here to go down the rabbit hole of the theory that at least some culture's deities are in fact demons, we will save that for another time. Instead, we would, again, like to draw some parallels between these "myths" and the events of this haunting.

To begin with, the horned serpents of these legends are known to drag people to watery deaths. While it may be speculation, who is to say that Daisy wasn't under the influence of such a spirit when she committed suicide? After all, these spirits are said to have the ability to hypnotize people. Another point of interest, is that these beings have the ability to shape-shift. Even Nancy herself suspected that the "demon" that haunted her home may be appearing as other things to lure her and her family in.

Furthermore, as Nancy writes, the team left her and John's home to help another family up the river. Drawing yet another parallel to the legend, the spirit of the horned serpent was known to travel the water-ways. Last, but certainly not least, the horned serpent is associated with the control of storms, and the day the paranormal team leaves, Western Kentucky was hit with one of the worst ice storms in its history. True, it may be a coincidence, but it would be one of many.

8. Native American Horned Serpents, Ibid
9. Native American Horned Serpents, Ibid

Concluding Thoughts

What we have presented to this point are the facts as recorded in Nancy's own words, and uncovered by our own efforts. As I stated previously, this book is mainly to showcase the hard work and courageous effort of Nancy. She was careful to keep a written record of events, and she and John both were warriors for staying in that house for so many years. In telling her story, my co-author and I hope to honor her memory, and fulfill her wish to provide inspiration to any who may find themselves in a similar story.

While no one can convince you besides yourself, we hope that between the stories, evidence, and the first-hand accounts, you will consider this which is before you. Consider, if you will, that we are between the light and dark, and where you dwell is up to you. As seen in her diaries, faith in the light, even when there was nothing but darkness, was one thing that enabled Nancy to fight for her home and family. We don't have to be perfect to have or practice our faith, especially as it is not always an easy thing. Even so, sometimes it is all we have.

We can hear some of you protesting, "when did this become a sermon?" Truly, this was always a sermon. Once the story has been heard, and the evidence examined, we must begin to consider. In considering, we begin to ask questions and search for something more. Slowly, we begin to unveil the truth, and once we know, we are bound by the knowledge. To fight it or turn away is a futile act. Even if you close your eyes, the truth will always be there. We may not fully be able to explain it, or like it, but it is the truth never-the-less. Reality is more than physicality. The only conclusion must be faith.

Bibliography

Contributors, Multiple. Lewis & Clark Corps of Discovery, 1803–1806: The Greatest Exploration in the Nation's History. Back Home In Kentucky, Inc., 2003.

"Native American Horned Serpents of Myth and Legend." Native Languages of the Americas, 1998–2020, https://www. native-languages.org/horned -serpent.htm

"Native American Legends: Sint-Holo." Native Languages of the Americas, 1998, www.native-languages.org/morelegends/sint-holo.htm.

Niemi, Ryan. "Wickliffe, Kentucky." Wickliffe, KY, Sunset Dynamics, 2008–2024, topoquest.com/place-detail.php?id=506708.

Society, Kentucky Historical. "Fort Jefferson Site." *Kentucky Historical Society*, Kentucky Historical Society, 2024, history.ky.gov/markers/fort-jefferson-site.

Subject 1, Interviewed by Blankenship and Johnson, 16 Oct. 2024

Subject 2, Interviewed by Blankenship and Johnson, 12 Nov. 2024

Survey, Kentucky Archaeological. "Wickliffe Mounds State Historic Site." *Discover Kentucky Archaeology*, Commonwealth of Kentucky, 2022, archaeology.ky.gov/Find-a-Site/Pages/ Wickliffe.aspx.